THE
RECRUIT

THE
RECRUIT

A Story of Faith, Miracles, and Divine Intervention

DAVID YANEZ

Banner Publishing

THE RECRUIT:
A Story of Faith, Miracles, and Divine Intervention
(Previously published as *My Military Life and the Power of God*.)

David Yanez Ministries
RevMedia Publishing
P.O. Box 5172
Kingwood, TX 77325
www.davidyanezministries.com
www.revmediapublishing.com

ISBN: 978-1-62911-209-1
eBook ISBN: 978-1-62911-210-7
Printed in the United States of America
© 2006, 2014 by David Yanez

Distributed by
Banner Publishing
1030 Hunt Valley Circle
New Kensington, PA 15068

DEDICATION

This book could only have been written by the gracious sacrifice of my wife, Irene, who gave me the time I needed to follow God's plan. She never questioned any plan, but only asked, when or where do we have to be? Irene, you have been beside me during the toughest of times. Your never-ending faith in me and in God gave me the strength and courage to keep believing. I could never be half the man of God I want to be without you. You complete me and the vision God has given us. You are a great wife, mother, and woman of God. I love you.

Thanks to our children, David, Nathaniel, Matthew, and Faith. You are the most precious gifts God could ever give me. I am proud of each one of you. I love ya'll.

This book would have not been possible without the great memories and friends aboard USS Lewis B. Puller (FFG-23). To the crew, I salute you. I also thank the veterans and current military in service today. It is an honor to call each one of you brother and sister. The dedication and danger you take daily for the countless millions depending on your protection is unbelievable. Without you, our freedom, liberty, and the very America that we all serve and love would be in jeopardy. I salute each one of you and thank you for the ultimate sacrifice you give for our country.

Finally, thanks to the men and women of God who opened their homes to me over the years. Each one of you blessed this young man of God tremendously. I thank you for making a stranger a friend.

SPECIAL THANKS

A special thanks to my mother Juanita Yanez Martinez. She stepped up to the plate of faith when God called my dad home in 1972. She was in her early twenties at the time with three kids to support. She had very limited help outside of her immediate family, but she was strong and raised us with God. I remember the prayers, the cries, and the joy of a young woman believing in God. And thanks to my second dad, Salvador Martinez, for taking a step of faith and marrying a single mother with three children. Thanks for being the best father God could have picked to care for His children.

CONTENTS

A Word from the Author 8

1. God Comes Knocking 9
2. God's Boot Camp 16
3. Lost in the Hospital 25
4. The Return of the Rev 35
5. That's Why They Call It Apprenticeship 41
6. Reporting For Duty 47
7. First Port Visit 52
8. Full Speed Ahead, Christians Aboard 57
9. Finding Friends and Family Outside the Base 62
10. Aloha, Baby. I Am Going to Hawaii 68
11. Sound the Alarm—Minister Went AWOL 74
12. Captain's Mast and the Sentencing of the Rev 83
13. Robbed at Sea 90
14. One Last Miracle Before I Leave 99

Conclusion 104

Where Is the Rev Now? 106

Military Support Information 109

Other Books by David Yanez 110

Salvation Prayer 111

Prayer for Healing 114

A WORD FROM
THE AUTHOR

I wrote this book to share my experiences about faith with you. I was a young man, just nineteen years old, when God told me to trust Him and join the United States Navy. I preached then and still preach today. While writing the book, I could literally see a map of my spiritual education throughout my entire enlistment. If I were to pray for one thing that you would get from reading this book, it would be to know that you are not alone in your walk. The Creator of heaven and earth is with you at all times. When God calls you, He will provide. Faith is a growing process in everyone's walk with God. We are told in the Bible that there are those with no faith, little faith, some faith, more faith, and great faith. I believe we can all attain great faith. This is a journey in my process hopefully to inspire you in your journey.

1

GOD COMES KNOCKING

I grew up in a Christian home in the downtown Houston area in the 1970s and '80s. My childhood was no different than most others. We had several things that were popular back then. Believe it or not, a VCR and cable meant you were a happening family. My parents showed us the importance of having God in our life and made sure we knew the responsibility that went with knowing Him. I remember one thing Mom would tell me—if you follow God you had better follow Him, no matter what! No excuses! Mom and Dad believed that if you served God your character would change that instant. That all things such as cursing, lying, smoking, drinking, and any other hang-ups you had would disappear the instant you found Jesus. If they didn't, that meant your commitment was not sincere. I know that seems impossible to some, but occasionally that kind of transformation happens. I know that the Holy Spirit is powerful and able to make a drunk or addict sober in minutes. But there are many times that a struggle with an addiction or habit may be a journey. I knew that eventually I would follow God with all my heart. My father was a minister who was extremely loved and very popular. He passed away when I was only one. My mom remarried when I was about five years old. For years, people told me that I would be an evangelist preaching around the world someday. Hearing that all the time, from childhood to my teens, would make one assume that it was definitely going to happen.

I attended Sweetwater Christian School beginning in the sixth grade and did the occasional reading of the Scriptures and mini-sermonettes for the class or chapel. The teachers picked me to do it, and I was obliged because I knew that one day preaching would be my vocation. I assumed that one day I would get tired of not following God and eventually change my life. That seemed simple enough. Right! I was never really a bad guy. I was into sports and that's really about it. My schoolwork was decent. I worked at a grocery store every day after school. After I graduated, I did the normal things everyone else did. I worked two jobs and tried to go to college. The only problem with that was that I liked working more than going to class. So I lost interest in college quickly; plus, I was trying to pursue one of my lifelong dreams—to be a professional soccer player in Europe.

When I was sixteen, I made the US Youth National Soccer team and was supposed to make the trip to Europe. I was planning to make it a one-way trip. I planned to stay over there until I made a European team or starve to death, whichever came first. But I never made the trip. I had no money. My parents couldn't afford to send me. It was $5,000 for a one-month trip, and soccer never had sponsors in the 1980s. I later got a letter that invited me to go to Europe with a team traveling in the spring of 1991. All I needed was the airfare, but they gave me no guarantees of making a team. I had time to save and was working hard to get the money I needed. But things started changing. I had no idea what God was about to do in me.

One day, while driving my bread delivery truck on my second job, a weird feeling came over me. I felt an overwhelming emptiness in me. I started crying for no reason at all. I arrived at my next stop and had to get myself together. Everybody was unloading products to take through the back door of a grocery store. At that moment, I ignored the empty feeling, figuring I could deal with it later. Later that night when I got home, I knew my life had to change and that I needed to get right with God. So I made a commitment to God that I would follow Him the best I could.

That lasted about a month. My cousins, friends, and brother were at the beginning of their clubbing days. I really didn't like going to nightclubs, but tagged along with them sometimes. I couldn't dance, didn't drink, and really didn't want to meet anyone at a bar. I figured that a godly woman wouldn't be there, so why should I look. Months went by, and I could not keep up with my commitment to God. I eventually let my indecisiveness get the best of my immaturity at work. I started getting frustrated and disappointed with myself, but blamed my job for all the emptiness in my life. Eventually, the bread company got tired of my excuses, gave me my paycheck, and asked me not to return the next day. Hey, that was a great job. I made $450 a week in the late 1980s. That is comparable to earning $650 a week today. Not bad for a guy just out of high school. But I let it get away.

The boss at my other job was also upset with me for calling in sick and even walking off once during a busy workday. I didn't realize it then, but now I do. God will get your attention when He wants to. I tried hanging with friends and family, but nothing seemed right. One day after working a long twelve-hour shift stocking groceries, I couldn't go to sleep. I had lain down on the sofa bed and finally fallen asleep after watching *An Officer and a Gentlemen* on the VCR. I woke up hearing my cat and dog fighting on the floor. I threw a pillow at them and tried to go back to sleep. After a few minutes, I realized that the dog and cat were not making noise anymore. That was something very unusual for them. I got off the sofa bed to check on them and saw something that baffles me even to this day. Both the dog and the cat were lying down quietly, side by side, staring at the closed bathroom door. I felt something was in the room and had a funny feeling inside of me. It was that same emptiness I had felt in the bread truck. It was back and stronger than before. I could also feel something behind the bathroom door that seemed to be drawing me in. I hesitated because of fear. (Plus, if something supernatural were in your bathroom, you'd probably want to make sure that they had finished their business before you opened the door.) I cracked open the bathroom door with one eye squinting, and I peeked in.

Nothing was in there. Relieved, I walked into the bathroom and instantly felt the presence of God. I started to cry and got on my knees. Looking up, I saw a miniature movie of my future life playing on one side of the bathroom mirror. I looked happy and had everything I ever wanted. I seemed to have been living a good life and my heart belonged to God. I had a soccer career overseas and had a nice family in this miniaturized movie. But I was still alone in my big house, sitting on my huge chair reading a Bible. I was crying because I was empty inside and I knew God had called me to preach the gospel. On the second half of the mirror, I could see all the people I would touch with the message of the gospel. I saw the power of God performing healings and miracles. There was something else I saw in that half of the mirror—the struggle and price for all this to come to pass. I looked deeper and deeper hoping to find an excuse not to take that route. But as I looked deeper, I found myself staring at myself in the mirror, nose to nose with my reflection. I backed up slowly. Disgust filled my heart. In the mirror, I saw the filth of sin all over me. I may not have drank, smoked, or used drugs, but I still had sin in my life. I had lived a good, clean life; I cared and believed in God. It didn't matter. Sin was sin. If you do not have Jesus as your Savior, you are a sinner. The Word of God says all have sinned and come short of the glory of God. Standing there, I saw what sin really was. It was dark, cold, and it quietly stood there in your life, not making a noise. Seeing this made me think. How could I go to Europe to play soccer knowing all this? I mean, the only road to take was predestined for me. Before I was born, a doctor told my mother that I was a tumor. An evangelist prayed over me, and declared that I was going to be a baby boy and to name me David. I was going to preach all over the world. Knowing there was only one real choice for me to make, I got on my knees and prayed to God. I asked Jesus to come into my heart. Since this was like the third or fourth time I had prayed this prayer, I added a few more lines to the sinner's prayer. Those few lines asked God to make me stronger and remove anyone in my life that would keep me from following Him.

After this, I just sat on the bathroom floor thinking about what just happened. Eventually I made it back to the sofa bed and fell asleep. The next morning, I noticed the dog and the cat were in the same position, side by side lying down. But this time they were in front of the sofa. Quickly I looked around and didn't feel or see anything unusual. But while stepping off the sofa bed, I felt the presence of God come into the room again. Bowing my head down and getting on my knees, I began to pray. A still, small voice began to speak. God said, "I want you to go into the navy."

I replied quickly. "God, I just came back to you and now you want to get me killed and take me home already?"

God told me He wanted me to join the navy today. I replied, "Yes Lord, but for how long?" I figured I might as well ask, since God was talking to me right then. God replied, "I only want you to join for two years." After the presence left, I started to wonder if all this was really happening. Reluctantly, I decided that this was definitely God giving me an order, not an option.

There was a recruiter about two miles from my apartment. I called and he said he had an appointment open for that morning if I would just drop in. I didn't have a car because my finances had gotten that bad. So I just decided to jog in. When the recruiter saw me breathing heavy and sweating, he got a little suspicious. He asked me what I was running from. He didn't believe me when I told him I wanted to join the navy and had jogged there from my apartment. I told him that I had talked it over with my father, and he had suggested that I join the navy for a couple of years. Well, if you know anything about military recruiters, they are very sly.

After getting my test scores on a pretest he kept telling me my test scores were good enough to get me into any job I wanted in the navy. I kept asking him about the two-year program and he kept pushing the four and six-year plan.

I began to learn a spiritual attribute that is so powerful. I stood on what God told me for the first time in my life. I asked the recruiter if I could have a few minutes to talk to my dad and ask his advice. He gave me permission to use his phone and then stepped out of the room.

I looked up to heaven and prayed a simple prayer, "Dad, you sent me to do this but this man is saying the four-year deal or six-year deal is what I qualify for. Please help me." I sat there for a brief moment until God replied to me, audibly, that I was to tell him the two-year deal contract is in the bottom right drawer of his desk, and that's the only one I would sign. I was so excited that God responded to my request so quickly.

The recruiter came back in and asked, sarcastically, if my dad was able to help me. I replied, "Yes. He said that the only deal I need to sign is in your bottom right hand drawer, or I don't sign at all." The recruiter was upset with me, but pulled the contract out. He replied by saying that he didn't know who my father was, but he didn't appreciate me going through his drawers. I just smiled. He calmed down and explained to me that the deal I was signing was not going to guarantee me a job title in the military, and that I was going to be placed on the ship as a bottom feeder. No rank. No rate. No designated job. I would probably have the hardest job and the most work on any ship I was assigned to during the entire two years. Disappointed, I told him I understood. (I had really wanted one of those officer uniforms.) According to the recruiter, I could leave anytime within a year for boot camp. I told him I wanted the next available date.

On May 5, 1991, I entered the military, embarking on a two-year voyage with God. Talk about trusting! I gave up everybody and everything in just three weeks. My family thought I was crazy. My friends asked if I was running from something or someone. My boss and coworkers thought that I had finally lost it and hit rock bottom. And wouldn't you know, on the same day that I was scheduled to leave for the military, my flight to Europe to play soccer was taking off as well.

While in the airport, we were left on our own recognizance to board the plane. They actually don't clamp down on you until you reach the shuttle to boot camp. There were four of us from Houston waiting to board the plane to San Diego. The other three were drunk and joked about skipping the plane. We had all heard stories from our recruiters about a couple of recruits who got so drunk that they ended up on the wrong plane. Eventually, they were found and dishonorably discharged. While the other guys horsed around, I looked out the terminal windows, wondering what God had in store for me.

As we boarded, I kept looking back. Thoughts kept pouring into my mind. All I had to do was turn around and go home. Did I really want to go into the navy? I confess that I was reluctant as I passed through the gate with one final thought: God, I am yours. Do what you need to do. Just take care of me and bring me back alive.

2

GOD'S BOOT CAMP

I slept through the flight, missing dinner. Back then, you actually had a decent meal on flights. Sleep, however, seemed more important to me than food. Knowing that boot camp was going to be eight weeks long, I figured they would feed me three meals a day. But sleep was not guaranteed to me, or anyone else. As the plane taxied to the arrival gate, my thoughts returned to what or who might be waiting for me in my new "home" in Los Angeles. Ever since I was a child, I understood who God was and that He knew my every thought. But since the trip to Los Angeles started, I could hear myself automatically conversing with Him.

Nobody was waiting for us. So, the four of us decided to go check out the scenery outside. We met up with some other guys who seemed lost, and sat at the curb outside baggage claim, staring at the night sky in silence. I think most of us were so quiet because we all thought the same thing. We should have brought more than $20 with us. If we had, we would have booked the next flight back home. The recruiters had instructed us to bring only the standard $20 to mail our civilian clothes home and buy essentials. The funny thing about that was that when my mom received my clothes back in the mail, she was shocked and thought the worse. I had managed to scribble a note on the inside of the box in huge letters that read, "I AM OKAY, JUST PRAY."

We sat on the curb for an hour and a half, my introduction to the military concept of hurry up and wait. Finally, a white van pulled up, its headlights glaring in our weary faces. A man stepped out and looked at each one of us. The first thing he said was, "I hope you are all here. If any one of you knows of anybody who has skipped out of this little powwow, you had better speak up." No one did. Then he gave a small role call, stating our last names and the cities where we had enlisted. On the ride to the base, I think we all realized that we had missed our final opportunity to get out.

Imagine a room filled with about one hundred and seventy-five guys who are totally unsure of what they had done, and even a little scared. That was what awaited me at the end of the ride to the airport. We were escorted into a room and were told to sit down and be quiet. Then it began. A man dressed in a khaki uniform ambled into the room and began yelling, "What did you bring me tonight? These are sorrier than last night's group!"

Next was another roll call. This time, when we heard our names, we were to give our social security numbers. The guy in khaki made a point to tell us to use only numeric values in relaying the information. I didn't get it until a guy sitting in front of me started to have problems. His name was Cory, and he would eventually become a good friend. He kept saying his social security number, but instead of zero, he would say the letter "O" and the people in charge got mad. Three times the petty officer got in his face and yelled at him. Cory was so nervous he didn't catch what he was doing wrong. I leaned forward just a little bit and whispered, "Say zero." He continued looking forward and this time repeated his social security number, using zero.

Each man was issued a number—either 147, 148, or 149—to separate us into groups. When 147 was called, thirty-five guys stepped forward and left the building to join the group that came in the night before. Then came number 148. I stepped forward along with eighty-four other guys. We left the building and officially became Recruit Company 148.

That night I got very little sleep before being awakened with trashcans banging and extremely bright halogen lights in my face. Recruit Company 148 spent the next four or five days getting our first issue of clothing (underwear, socks, and sweats), getting inoculations, and our navy haircuts—shaving us bald. We later had a little session with men posing to be from the secret service. These men claimed they knew who we were and that we were hiding out under alias names. Time to confess! I mean, who would believe that stuff? (You would be surprised!) They found drug dealers, felons, and illegal immigrants that slipped by the system. After that interrogation and a urinalysis to test for drug use, our group was cut down to about sixty-five. We were put into the hands of two company commanders (drill instructors) who would have us, body, mind, and soul for the next eight weeks.

These two company commanders were the first people we saw in the morning and the last we saw at night. They were there to get inside our heads and push us to the limit. They hand-picked a small group of guys who were given titles: recruit petty officer (RCPO), master-at-arms, yeoman, assistant master-at-arms, and assistant yeoman. I knew these guys had already been picked by the company commander ahead of time. Over the weeks of boot camp, these jobs changed hands according to our successes or failures in training.

I tried to get to know the guys in my company, but we hardly had time to talk to one another. We were constantly watched, even when doing pushups and marching. Why does a sailor need to learn how to march? Aren't we going to be on a ship most of the time? Plus, we weren't the smartest marching group on base. One day we were standing in formation in front of the exchange (convenient store). Another company commander from a different unit came out and called us to attention. We obliged by marching off to his commands. He parked us under a bridge for about an hour until we got smart and knew we were in trouble. We double-timed it back, trying to follow all the rules, hoping not to be noticed that we didn't have a company commander walking with us back to our barracks. But when we got there, our company commanders were furious. They made us put everything we had on into our lockers, including our winter jackets, gloves, and night-watch caps. He marched us around outside until our faces became red. Then he exercised us to death. He called it "hot wiring" a unit. That mistake never happened again.

Because of the mistake, someone needed to take the fall for our failure, and this time it was the master-at-arms. So the current position was vacated and someone needed to fill it. Everybody in the group put up his hand and volunteered, except me. Our commander picked his new master-at-arms and introduced two new positions that needed volunteers.

Our company visited the recruit chapel services that first Sunday after our arrival. Most of the guys went just to get out of quarters and have something to do. The two new jobs that needed to be filled were the religious petty officers (RPO)—one Catholic and one Protestant. I pondered if I should volunteer for this or not. The odds of him picking me weren't that good. He paced across the top of the table, which looked like a picnic table that stretched through the middle of the sixteen quarters and served as a divider. Before he got to me he asked, "Who wants to be RPO? You will pray for these guys and for any emergencies that come up." He first asked for a Catholic volunteer. Then he asked for a Protestant volunteer. I picked my hand up as he stared at the desperate faces who wanted to have some type of job. He passed me, still looking at the sea of hands. "Yanez, you're it!" He turned around without looking at me and left for the night.

God knew this boot camp would be His boot camp for me as a minister. This opportunity was better than any seminary or on-the-job training. I was surrounded by people from all over the country, locked up and under pressure every day. If someone needed a clean slate, this was the place to get it. Nobody knew who you were before this. I didn't realize it then, but now I know that this was the best place for me.

As a religious petty officer, I prayed every night for the recruits before hitting our racks (beds). The Catholic guy took the first night. His prayer was beautiful and everybody received it. It was almost poetic. The next night was my turn. Before I prayed, I went and hid in the showers. Since nobody used them at night, I figured that this would be my prayer closet. I asked God to help me give these guys a feeling of peace.

I returned to my rack and faced the men. I asked, "Please bow your heads." My prayer was simple. "Father, I ask that each one of us would be given your peace. Let us know that our families are being taken care of and that our finances will be met. Father, we love you and ask for your strength for tomorrow. Amen."

From that time forward, the guys looked at me differently. In one of our training classes, one of the guys told me he felt something when I prayed. I was amused when the Catholic people asked the Catholic RPO not to pray anymore. They wanted me to pray every night. The prayers became so successful that a few of the guys came to me asking me to pray for them individually. Most of these prayers were for family, for release from fear, and to succeed. As the weeks went on, I was often awakened in the middle of the night to pray for family emergencies, fears, comfort, and many other requests. At the time, I didn't realize what these guys were doing. Now I understand that they were bonding to my faith in God. I believe they saw a young man who generally cared about their needs and loved God. This image became a staple in my early ministry.

Mail call was the most interesting time for all of us. We would get our mail on Friday (so we could have something to think about over the weekend). Sometimes guys would get "Dear John" letters from girlfriends. I sat with these heartbroken men and prayed with them. Usually, they would get over it. I tried to encourage them by reminding them that we were in this program for eight weeks and that God knew all about the situation and the timing. Then I would tell them that you can't do anything about it until you get out, so the best thing to do until then is pray. Pray and concentrate on the task at hand, which for all of us was getting to recruit graduation day.

During the third week of boot camp, we were allowed to make one two-minute phone call. No one knew if the person he was calling would be home. If not, too bad. In the eighties, nobody had cell phones as you see today. And if no one answered, we had to leave a message on an answering machine.

Typically, we all used a telephone booth that sat in the middle of a parking lot (weird). Our first call had to be made collect. Imagine a line with seventy-five people staring at you and waiting for their turn on one phone. I think only half the people who made calls actually found someone home. Half of those didn't get through because their families wouldn't accept the charges. Hey, long distance back then was expensive! We were charged 65 to 85 cents a minute, plus a $2.50 connection charge, and that was nighttime charge. Usually we had to make these calls in the morning or afternoon. That meant higher per-minute charges and connection charges. Long distance back then was like a bad word, and so it's no wonder families said no to collect calls.

Anyway, that first call took its toll on the recruits. That night, I was asked to speak to them in lieu of the normal prayer before lights out. I shared with them about Jesus' illustration of the lost sheep and how the shepherd left the ninety-nine to go find the one that was lost. I told them how excited he was about finding that one lost one. I went on to illustrate that even though the ninety-nine were left behind, they were safe and secure. The one that was lost needed the attention and care of the shepherd. Our families were safe, secure, and most likely praying for us. We were the ones needing the care of the Great Shepherd. So our energies should be directed to our own safety and well-being, and with helping the Great Shepherd find us.

After this devotional, many men asked me to start a Bible study group on our weekday off time. I agreed. We had a couple of hours of free time here and there to write, talk, and do whatever as long as we stayed in quarters. Free time was a precious commodity. I was amazed that these recruits would want to spend time in the Word of God.

After the fourth week or so, we were all relaxed and comfortable with one another. That's when I began to hear criticism from other recruits with different religious backgrounds. There was an atheist, a Buddhist, and a Muslim. It sounds like the beginning of a joke, but it wasn't. They all argued that God was different and that Jesus was not the Son of God. I led them through several Scriptures that proved Jesus was indeed the Son of God. Since I only had the New Testament with me, I couldn't cover any of the prophecies. The atheist said we all survive on positive energy and that I had very positive energy, more than others had. I told him it was because I was baptized by the Holy Spirit. That positive energy was the power of God in me. He freaked and left me alone. The Buddhist said that we must continue to work with each other and agree that the Spirit of God is in everything and everyone. If we lived a good life, Buddha would help us no matter what. I told him that God's Spirit was in everything, but that Jesus has always been. He was there during the day of creation, sitting with God. The Scriptures show God telling Jesus, *"Let us make man in our image*" (Genesis 1:26). Then I took him to the gospel of John and showed him the Scriptures about Jesus. (See John 1:1, 3.) In the beginning was the Word and the Word was with God, and the Word was God...all things were made by Him and without Him was not anything made that was made. That stumped him, and he left me alone from then on as well. I hate arguing with people about the Word. I still dislike it, so I try to avoid it as much as possible. Funny thing is that now most confrontations I have are not with other religions, but with Christians. Some people want the Bible to say what they want so they can keep living the way they want without conviction.

The Muslim wanted me to stop praying for him in Jesus' name. I told all of them that Jesus will be there for them when they were ready. I was really spunky back then. I probably could have been less abrasive, but again, I was learning.

Most of the time, I would have to find something in the New Testament to validate a point. We had been issued tiny Bibles with only the New Testament and Psalms. It was all I had, so I worked with it the best I could. I read my little Bible, cover to cover, countless times during boot camp.

About the fifth week, one of the recruits received devastating news. I was standing at my rack, folding clothes, when someone yelled out my name. "Yanez, Yanez come quickly!" I ran to see what was happening. I saw our yeoman on the floor, crying and crying. I asked the guys standing around him what was going on. One replied, "You need to pray for him and his wife. His wife just had a miscarriage and she is in the hospital in San Antonio." I stood motionless for a few seconds, wondering what in the world do you tell someone in this situation. I mean, my faith was growing, but what could I say? The only thing I could do is embrace the yeoman and say, "God will take care of your child, my friend, and your wife." I went on to tell him that we all loved him and would pray for him. But there was a time to weep, and now was that time. We all cried. That was the first time I felt completely helpless and at a loss for words.

Our yeoman was granted a couple of days plus a weekend to visit his wife. Every night that he was gone, we prayed for them. That sparked an interest in asking for prayer requests every night, which became our practice.

The yeoman came back recharged and ready to finish the rest of training. We needed our yeoman; he was the one that would write our medical slips. So we were glad to have him back. He did have the option to get out or to come back later, but he wanted to finish with us. We were happy to see him so positive. We knew God had answered our prayers for him and his wife. He came back just in time for the recruit Olympics between navy and marines. We went over to the marine training camp where they were all kneeling on their hands and barking like dogs. They pretty much creamed us in everything except soccer and basketball.

3

LOST IN THE HOSPITAL

We were one big happy unit—working together with just a few more weeks until graduation. We were in our sixth week, which was our special assignment week. I was assigned to work on the mess decks in Galley 5. About fifteen hundred recruits ate three times a day, every day of the week. So to help the mess chief, each company sent half their crew to the galley for different shifts on the sixth training week. I worked lunch and dinner, which was cool because I could sleep in, do some exercise, then head to the galley to eat lunch and then serve it. I skipped breakfast because I knew I could eat as much as I wanted for lunch and dinner.

I had fun picking on the new recruits and teasing them with stories—just as I had been teased my first night on base. I also teased the newly shaved guys who were fresh out of the barbershop, or the butcher shop, as we called it. You only had your hair shaved off completely once. This is to make everyone look the same—nobody different from the next guy. Same clothes and same hair cut. But after that, we could tell the barbers how much we wanted off the sides and top.

The hardest work in the galley was the scullery, which was cleaning all those dishes. That's why I have a dishwasher now. I cleaned enough pots, pans, plates, and silverware to last a lifetime. People are so disgusting about how they eat and what they do to their food. It's nasty. I got out of the scullery the first day. The chief had seen me restocking plates, bowls, and silverware and handing it to the recruits, and he liked the idea. I was moving the line quicker by handing them everything instead of waiting for them to figure it out. That became my new assignment. I also got a couple of extra phone calls home courtesy of the chief for the hard work.

Another perk of having galley duty was when we finished our jobs, we could sneak off and take naps. I would eventually find out that was a popular thing to do throughout the navy. Don't believe half the shows you see on the military. I have seen a whole bunch of them too. None are true. Thirty percent of the time is used doing our jobs, and it's very formal. Twenty percent is spent skating (hiding and napping). The other fifty percent is spent complaining, handing work off to someone else, or saying I am not doing that until you finally waste enough time and it's 4:15 and liberty calls! We frequently snuck into the attic of the galley to take naps in between lunch and dinner. The chief eventually caught us and gave us extra duty as punishment. Those extra duties consisted of cleaning the windows with a 3-inch squeegee and washing the front concrete with a bar of soap and a brush.

One day during my sixth week, I was folding my laundry back at the quarters when one of the guys asked, "Does that hurt?" I looked at him, puzzled, and replied that I felt fine. He then pointed to my neck. I felt my neck and something was different. I headed to the mirror by the company commander's office. What I found surprised me. I had a huge lump on the right side of my neck. I couldn't explain it. The lump hadn't been there the night before or even an hour before. It was almost the size of a large grapefruit and extremely hard. It literally looked like I had a softball stuck in my neck.

I was scared and went immediately to the company commander's door. As soon as I knocked, I heard a mean, "What?"

"Sir, it's Yanez" I answered.

"So...," the commander replied.

"I think you should see this" I urged.

He answered, "Yanez, this better be..." He opened the door and jumped back yelling, "Oh my God! What happened?"

I told him that I had just discovered the lump and needed to go to medical. He yelled for the yeomen to get me a request form and take it to medical. I headed out to medical not knowing what to expect. It was a long walk—all the way to the other side of the recruit training base. The military uses different colored lines painted on the floor to direct us to the destination of choice. For medical, the color was white. So all I had to do was follow the white line all the way to medical. Sounds simple, but at night with no moonlight and no street lights the yellow, white, and gray all looked the same. We all had our own stories of getting lost at night coming back from a marching party (exercising us to death by a SEAL trainer as punishment).

My company commander noticed the problem with the lines and called in a base shuttle van to get me to medical quickly. He wasn't sure what was wrong with me and wanted to make sure that I made it to medical in a timely fashion. Any time one of us had medical or dental, we would wander around so we could waste as much time as possible away from the company.

I sat at the curb and about an hour later the shuttle finally arrived. I would have been dead if it had been an emergency. Medical was a large clinic that handled all the recruits on the base. They treated "crew crud" most the time. Crew crud described what happened when you get a bunch of recruits from all different parts of the country and lock them up together. Eventually, a strand of bacteria unfamiliar to others' immune systems will make some recruits sick for no apparent reason. Medical treated each new case of crew crud with pills and IVs when they could. It would usually clear up in a few days. Our company never got it, but we did get a lot of injuries and stuff like that. The staff at medical was familiar with us for that reason. As soon as I told the triage desk I was from company 148, the duty officer asked me what was wrong this time. I was put in a room and asked a series of questions like: what had I eaten, where did I sleep, did I have a history of similar lumps. The corpsman didn't know what the problem was. He said I needed to go to Balboa Hospital so a specialist could look at it.

Again, I sat out in the parking lot to wait for the base shuttle to take me to the hospital. I had only seen the outskirts of San Diego (San Dog) when we arrived at the airport that first night of boot camp. The shuttle driver was pretty cool; he offered to take me through McDonald's. When I told him I didn't have any money, he said that was too bad. Hey, at least he asked.

We headed up the long hill into the entrance of the Balboa Naval Hospital, a beautiful facility on the top of a green, tropical setting typical of San Diego. Being only in the service for six weeks, I couldn't remember all the insignias and ranks. I got the salutes outside the hospital completely wrong. I was pulled over three times before getting in the door of the hospital for not saluting properly. Anyway, I blamed it on my swollen neck. They all forgave me and said to get inside.

Part of the navy experience is constantly having people riding us or getting in our heads. The purpose was to get us mentally ready for the most catastrophic situations. The hospital triage was extremely busy that night. Several marines in civilian clothes were covered in blood pouring from their foreheads. People complained about the time it took to see a doctor. Finally, the corpsman came to visit me. He asked if he could take a sample from my neck with a huge needle. I had to agree—I needed help! He broke three needles before he got a sample of anything. I saw blood but didn't feel pain at all. He said that was good and bad.

The corpsman decided I should be admitted so a specialist could see me the next morning. If I had known I was going to be checked into the hospital, I would have brought some money to hit the McDonald's the hospital had in the basement. I had left my money in my locker. We received partial paychecks every two weeks, but not more than $50 at a time. To compensate, they gave us vouchers to use at the exchange for phone cards, soap, etc... One of the recruits in our company tried to use his voucher at the base McDonald's during a medical visit. I didn't blame him. Our company commander made us march in front of McDonald's every morning so he could get his coffee. We could smell the food cooking and see all the people eating inside. He further humiliated us by making us march to the McDonald's parking lot to stand at attention and sing the Big Mac song. You know—two all-beef patties, special sauce... on a sesame seed bun. It's a good thing we didn't carry cash with us because we probably would have mobbed McDonald's.

I rested that night in my private-room bed on the third floor. I was able to watch TV for the first time in six weeks. I didn't even think of using the phone near my bed for fear of getting in trouble. I got there so late that I missed chow, but I learned a new word in the military scene called "mid-rations." The hospital kitchen served leftovers and quick fixes for people working overnight. Since I was in recruit training, I just showed my ID and told them my room number. That's the one thing I thought was cool about the navy. No matter what base or hospital you were at, you could pretty much pull into any galley and eat free. At least I did. I ate in Balboa Naval Hospital, Miramar Air Station, Pearl Harbor, Seattle Base, San Francisco Base, Long Beach Naval Station, countless Coast Guard stations, and even the Canadian Royal Naval Station in British Columbia, Canada.

I chowed down my mid-rations and headed back to my room. On the way, I passed by a room where a marine staff sergeant was yelling at a marine recruit. The staff sergeant tore the TV out of the wall and yanked the phone out of its receptacle. He told the marine recruit that he needed to look straight into the little hole in the ceiling during his entire hospital stay. Thank God I was in the navy. I hadn't seen my company commander there yet. In fact, my company commander never did come to see me.

It took the medical staff about two days of testing me to figure out that I needed surgery to remove this thing in my neck. It wasn't a swollen lymph node but was a cyst of some sort stuck on the outside of my neck in between my skin and nerves. By this time, I was enjoying my stay at the hospital. I had breakfast, lunch, dinner, and mid-rations everyday at the hospital galley. Everything was great until the third day when my doctor came to see me. He asked me to sit down so he could talk to me. He went on to say that the surgery was going to be very complicated. The grapefruit thing was tangled around the nerves in my neck and posed a significant threat. He was concerned about it crushing my windpipe. He had decided to wait one more day to see if it would untangle itself. If not, I would have to go straight to surgery. Since the lump was in my neck and tangled, I could lose certain movement in my nervous system, including the ability to walk, talk, and move freely. I could also die if they cut the wrong nerves. I listened to the doctor, and then asked if I could use the phone to call my mom. She didn't even know I was in the hospital.

I had taken the bad news like a man, but as soon as I started talking to my mom, I started crying. The doctor took the phone from me and explained the severity of the surgery to her. He handed me the phone, and by then I was a bit calmer. My sister's friend in Houston, Maurice, who was a great guy, paid for her, my nephew, and Mom to catch the morning flight to San Diego a day later. I was scheduled for surgery a day after talking to my mom. I was confined to my bed and they hooked up IVs and regulated what I ate. I sat in my bed and prayed, asking God to help me all day. My aunts and my dad called me to pray during the afternoon. But other than that, I was on my own.

The evening before surgery I was watching the ministers on television. That night I called every minister on television. I called toll free, used my calling card, and on the rare ones, called collect. Not one of them picked up. They were all busy. There must have been a huge altar call in heaven that day. I gave up after three hours when I ran out of calling card credits. I fell asleep reading my Bible.

In the middle of the night a nurse woke me up when she was checking my IV. She was so beautiful, and she was an officer.

"Is this your Bible? I found it on the floor."

I nodded and she put the Bible on my chest. I told her about the surgery and that I believed that God would heal me. She said that she knew I was going to be touched by God. She also said that she must have been sent to pray for me that night. The nurse prayed a simple prayer that the God of heaven and earth would touch me. She told me she went to a church called Cross on the Hill.

I closed my eyes and was awakened again, but this time not by the beautiful nurse. It was a completely different nurse. She yelled at me, "Who messed with your IVs?"

"The other nurse—the officer. She was very beautiful," I responded.

"I am the only nurse on this floor tonight," she replied, "and we don't have any officer nurses. I am as pretty as they get, son." She told me to hold on as she picked up the rails to my bed. An aide came to help her push my bed down the hospital corridor.

"What's going on?" I asked.

The nurse looked at me and replied, "Just keep quite. We need to operate on you immediately."

"But I'm not scheduled for another two hours. What about my family? My mom and sister are supposed to be here in another hour or so."

"Can't wait for that," she responded. "We will bring them to the waiting room. Don't worry."

The next stop was the operating room. Several nurses and doctors stared at me for what seemed like hours. I really thought things were getting bad and I started getting scared. Then everything just went black.

Later I learned I was under for about thirty minutes. When I opened my eyes, a doctor was sitting beside me. He welcomed me back. He began asking me questions about my mobility—if I could move my feet. I moved them. He asked me to move my lips and say hello. I did. He then asked if I could move my ears. I did, which made him jump back! I explained that I have always been able to do that. Then the doctor shared the amazing thing that had happened.

During the night, the grapefruit reduced to the size of a quarter. What remained was no longer hard or tough. In fact, it was jelly-like as it untangled from my around my nerves. That was the reason for the emergency surgery. They didn't want to give it a chance to grow back. The doctor explained that after he made his incision, whatever it was "jumped" out of my neck. He had caught it with a pan sitting next to the surgery table.

The doctor reached behind him and picked up a silver container. "Do you want to see it?"

How could I refuse? In the pan, I saw a roundish, slimy, black thing floating in some fluid. There was a little bit of white on the top surface, and it almost looked like it had tentacles. Whatever it was, I know that God made sure that it was not welcome in my body anymore. Amen!

Because the mass had come out of my neck with such force, the wound was large and it left a scar that I still have today. It's a small scar, but it itches when it's cold outside. I initially lost some feeling in that part of my neck, but the nerves eventually grew back and most of the feeling has returned.

My family had arrived early and went to my room, only to find it empty. My mom asked the closest nurse what had happened to me.

"I'm sorry" the nurse replied, "he's already gone." They all started crying! My mom almost lost it. The nurse quickly explained, "You misunderstood. He just got finished in surgery and is doing fine."

When I finally made it to my room, I had a great time visiting with Mom, my sister, and my nephew. God had moved miraculously for me. I had a couple days of recovery and checkups. This allowed time for the anesthesia chemicals to pass through my system. One thing I did learn the hard way was to eat the hospital food only. My sister brought me a quarter-pounder with cheese, after I had pestered her past her ability to refuse me. I tried chowing it down, but threw it all up immediately.

My mom, nephew, and sister decided to stick around an extra week to see my graduation. I thought that was cool. I couldn't wait to get back to my company. The doctor told me that I could go back to training only if I stood on light duty. I agreed, and he said he would get the papers ready for me to check out that afternoon. My mom and sister headed to their hotel and left me a number to contact them with the graduation ceremony information.

After they left, I found out some disturbing news. A nurse said that if I missed more than five days with my company, I would have to drop back to a different company in order to meet the time requirement for the basic training. I had missed half of my sixth week and half of my seventh. That was more than five days including weekends. I prayed, asking God why I would go through this only to lose my company. I believed we had something moving there. Then, I did something I had begun to do early in life and still do today. I left the situation in God's hands.

4

THE RETURN OF THE REV

An orderly wheeled me downstairs to the duty desk to give my papers to the clerk, who reminded me that most likely I would have to go back a week to a different company. He did say that it was up to the duty chief at the base.

The base shuttle van soon arrived, and as we started on our way, the driver began to talk about the duty chief. He told me the guy was crazy and quick tempered, and to just hand him my papers and keep my mouth shut. When we arrived at the building, the sun was setting just like in a movie. I entered cautiously and handed my papers to the duty chief without speaking, just as the driver had coached me.

The duty chief scanned my papers then looked up. Staring into my face he remarked, "So, did you miss more than a week?"

Before I could even open my mouth to reply, six or seven people came in to the office, laughing and playing. He got so furious with them, he forgot about me. After scolding these other recruits, he noticed me still standing silently.

"What are you still doing here?" he growled.

"I want to go back to my company, sir."

"Then go back to your division." He stamped my papers "Return to division on light duty." I was so excited—until I had to figure out how to get back to my division in the dark.

Thank God for the painted lines. I followed the (colored) line straight to the division building. The division is where all the company commanders had a meeting room, lounge, office, and racks to sleep. We would stand post in this building for a few hours at a time. It was okay duty. While others were on work parties, I stood in air conditioning, answered the phones, did a little paperwork, and made a couple of quick, unauthorized phone calls. I think part of the thrill of the military was seeing what you could get away with.

The medicine had left me feeling a little unbalanced, but I finally made it upstairs to check in. One of my friends was on watch. He was as excited to see me as I was to see him. The division officer came out and told us to cut the chitchat then directed me to wait in the lounge.

I sat there for about five minutes when the door going to the catwalk opened. The catwalk was a small walkway like a balcony that ran on the outside of the building. My company commander came walking through the door. He asked if I was feeling okay. I told him well enough to finish and graduate. He looked at my paperwork, smirked, and told me to follow him. We went across the catwalk to some private doors that led to his office, which was on the same floor as our quarters. He asked me to wait in his office for a few minutes while he went inside the quarters. I was surprised because he usually threw all of us out of his office. Only the yeoman and his minions were able to hang with him, eat pizza, and drink sodas. Too bad RPOs weren't included, because I sure could have used a pepperoni pizza around the third week.

My company commander came back through the door. He told me to head into the quarters. Just before we entered, the company commander put everybody at attention. As soon as I was in the room, he turned and left.

A thunderous burst of applause shook the quarters. Every recruit that had been standing at attention came out of formation clapping and hugging me. The guys began sharing, one by one, how they had missed me and my prayers. A few told me that they had never prayed before, believing that they would receive an answer. But they tried this one time—praying for me to return and believing that I would not be sent back a week. They were excited because God answered their request!

The Muslim told me that he decided to pray for me in Jesus' name. He did, and the next day, there I was. He now questioned his Muslim faith. The Buddhist said the same thing. But said he was angry with Buddha, because he didn't answer his request about me. The atheist said he had never, ever prayed before in his entire life, but he had yelled out to God that if he was real, then show himself by bringing Yanez back. He admitted that God might just be after all. At least that was a start.

The recruits also shared that they got tired of the Catholic RPO praying the same prayers every night. They didn't want to replace me as RPO, so they all took turns leading prayer for each thing they did. When I started as RPO for our company, we only prayed before going to bed. But as I led, I prayed for events such as shooting range, physical, meals, and anything we as a company felt we needed favor on. I was touched that they all stepped up and prayed in my absence.

Standing for God is never easy, and it's especially hard in a place like the military. So much in training was geared to a sexually explicit, vulgar, disgusting, and perverted mentality. I am sure that the navy and military as a whole changed when women began to serve duty aboard ships and go into combat. When I was in, women weren't allowed aboard ship or out to sea, with the exception of USS Prairie, a supply ship. They also had the highest pregnancy rate among female sailors.

Half the language used for training was sexually biased and suggestive. I don't want to share any training words or phrases in this book. I just want to point out that there was a certain conflict and pressure on anyone that stood for God in the military. But that was the point of my military life. Either I served God or I didn't. There was no in between, because the crew could see right through me. They saw my life every day. How I woke up, went through the day, handled the same pressures, and went to bed. They saw my reactions, good or bad, during the most trying times together.

Getting back in gear with training after sitting in a bed for a week was no easy task. You know that out-of-sync feeling you get when you go back to work or school the first day after being out sick? Multiply that times ten because of the drugs during surgery mixed with marching. The doctor gave me a light duty note, but in the military, that "light" was left up to interpretation. I did some marching but sat out on drills, and I didn't have to exercise. It was awkward, because my entire company would be dropped on the hot black top to push to China (pushups) and I got to just stand there in parade rest (relaxed stance). In fact, after one week, I think it got to some of the recruits. I also didn't have to wait in the chow line. Nor was I subject to surprise inspections. I guess because inspections go along with exercise. When you failed inspection, you had to work out until you dropped on the spot, or you were invited to the grueling marching party at night, or both. I needed to pay extra attention to tasks like getting notes to go to medical, catching up with necessary assignments to graduate, and I couldn't move fast enough to keep up with everyone else. I felt like I was going to pop a stitch on my neck if I walked too quickly. I also had to go take my picture for the Anchor (navy boot camp yearbook). For that, I took off my bandage because that would have looked scary on my mug shot. But I didn't know I had a huge purple bruise on my neck left over from the operation, and it showed up on my picture. The Anchor had pictures of our march through the parade, and there was a picture from behind with half my neck covered by a bandage.

We finally made it to graduation day. It was the Fourth of July weekend, so our graduation would be extra special with fireworks and added events. We had just had our USO Recruit Family Night, which brought many families and friends back together after an eight-week separation. I had already seen my mom and sister at the hospital, so it wasn't too tearful for me. But grown men do cry and cry they did. Fathers hugging their kids, husbands hugging wives, young men hugging moms and dads—it was nice. Nevertheless, we couldn't leave with our families until after graduation the next morning.

That night back in quarters, the air crackled with excitement. We knew we had made it. But we also knew we would probably never see each other ever again. We had made it as a team, but more than that, as friends.

The company commander came in and stepped across the top of the desk as he always did. "Let us pray," he said.

Usually, that was my cue. I started to pray my last prayer with these guys when he stopped me. "I have this one," he said, and began to pray for all of us. Afterward, he shared with me that he doesn't often pray for the graduating recruits, but he felt he had to that time. I thank God for my boot camp and experience in trusting Him, especially when He was all I had. I was nineteen years old and loved God and still love Him today.

We marched our best ever at graduation and won the marching award. It was an exciting day and an end to a trying eight weeks. After graduation and throwing our covers (hats) in the air, we marched back to the quarters one last time as Company 148. When we got upstairs, we went straight to our racks to see our new orders. Most of us sat or stood next to our beds and opened the envelopes in silence. Others didn't bother and just ran out the building to take advantage of the liberty time. I already knew my future. While others would go straight to leave (vacation) for fifteen days, then go to schools for another six to sixteen weeks in various places, I and a handful of other recruits would be in apprenticeship school for the next three weeks, then have leave for fifteen days. That meant we had only a four-day holiday weekend off and then report to class at 0800 hours on Monday.

Instead of dashing off to be with our families, we had to wait, and then go together to the training quarters. We had to check in, get meal passes, racks, and lockers. Men exiting the apprenticeship program told me to pick a top rack, but all the top racks were taken. I will explain in the next chapter why that was so important. Eventually, I was reunited with my family and had some real food for a change—you know, the fatty stuff or the good stuff, as I call it.

Surviving eight weeks of basic training showed me that I wasn't alone in this thing God had asked me to do. He gave me favor both with man and with Him.

5

THAT'S WHY THEY CALL
IT APPRENTICESHIP

At 0800 Monday morning, I reported to class with a few friends from boot camp. We were mixed in with companies that had graduated a week earlier, those who graduated at the same time, and some who had failed apprenticeship training. There were three types of apprenticeship: airman, fireman, and seaman—all bottom-of-the-barrel workers. I was a seaman. We did stupid stuff like paint the ship, scrub bilges, and all the other work nobody wanted to do. Seamen also pulled in the ship as deck hands, stood lookout watches, and drove the ship. They gave the least important guy the responsibility to steer the vessel. Crazy as it sounds, I was pretty good at it. But that part of the story comes later.

Apprenticeship was different from boot camp. We were not isolated from "life" as we were in boot camp. It was more or less like a crash course of navy college. We all had to be in class, but nobody was going to help us get there. Getting to class on time was up to each apprentice. We all had responsibilities for our quarters, such as cleaning and standing watch. Standing watch was a pain in the butt—four hour shifts around the clock. Somebody was always responsible for the watch list, and we usually kept to it. The hardest watch was the mid-watch, from 2400 to 0400. It was impossible to get enough sleep, no matter how hard we tried. We went to chow on our own, we were on liberty as long as we didn't have duty, and we didn't have a curfew. Besides all that, we were free to leave the base whenever we wanted to. Looking back, it was my indoctrination to military life at a base.

Our first day was filled with orientations by chief of quarters, counselors, meeting our instructor, and getting the agenda for the next three weeks. After apprenticeship training, we would be welcomed into the fleet and graduate from training. We needed to pass five academic tests.

The chief of quarters drilled us on not coming back to quarters so drunk that we might unconsciously pee on a shipmate, thinking we were in the head. They drilled this into the heads of the apprentices so much that it happened at least once with every class. Unfortunately, it happened to a friend of mine from boot camp, and the reason I know this is because he peed on me.

I was asleep on my bottom rack, dreaming of waterfalls. For some reason I woke up and saw a stream flowing my way—barely missing my body but drenching my rack. Then I heard someone yelling—my good friend who was standing watch. "He just peed on Yanez!"

I couldn't believe my bad luck. I thought to myself "I should have taken a top rack." (After that night, everybody moved to any available top rack.) The watch rover didn't want to make the report about the guy who peed in his sleep, but if he didn't, he knew I would be the one to get in trouble for having a wet rack. We woke up the chief on duty, whose quarters were downstairs, and he was livid. He yelled at the pee-pee guy who was drunk and in denial, but we had many witnesses. The dude kept yelling at me and screaming, "Why are you doing this to me, Yanez? You are supposed to be a man of God!" Mix in some occasional cursing and you get the idea.

I headed to the showers and the same chief on duty then got in my face. Showers were closed after 2100 every night. I told him I was the one peed on, and I needed a shower. He told me to make it quick. Now you know how important those watch rover's are to the system. I would have had a difficult time explaining all this without a witness.

I really think the poor drunk guy was baited—almost brain-washed. Every day and night, the chief of the quarters would tell us not to pee on our shipmates. Eventually, one of them would do it. Not to remove blame from the pee-pee man; he was responsible for his actions.

In the morning, I was embarrassed to sit in class. The pee-pee man was not there. He was in holding getting sober. I could tell everyone wanted to crack up. A day later, he was back in class and apologized to me about the incident in front of everybody. That was cool. I was glad to have that incident behind me. Or did I?

On the last week of training, a messenger came in to class and handed a note to our instructor. The message was for me—to report to the CO (commanding officer) for Captain's Mast (kind of like court). This CO was head of the entire training center. I followed the lines on the floor to his office. His line was gold for base command. I entered the room and saw pee-pee man standing at attention facing a desk. The CO sat behind his desk starring down pee-pee man. The CO welcomed me and asked me some questions. I confirmed the incident while at attention. The CO told me he was surprised by my restraint not to hurt this pee-pee man. He said he would have thrown him over the side of the ship or cut him with his knife. He was serious. He also told me to keep doing what I was doing, because he heard good things about me from boot camp and training. He dismissed me and I went back to class.

Pee-pee man finally understood the penalty for that urination. He lost rank, forfeiture of pay, and any school promised. That was sad about the school; he was supposed to go to a legal assistant school after training. The only reason he was at the apprenticeship training was that his school wasn't supposed to start for five weeks.

Three weeks training and two weeks leave would have set him up nice.

I had some other memorable times that were good. A couple of my friends, Cory and Thomas, from boot camp were also in training. We met at the chow line for lunch and hung out here and there. I went off base to check out San Diego. I wanted to find a church I could visit on Sundays. One thing I wanted to do was visit the church where the nurse at the hospital said she attended. I never could find it. Getting around town was difficult without a car.

During our orientation, we were told to travel in pairs. A military bashing had occurred outside the base so traveling in numbers made sense. I went to Sea World, San Diego Zoo, Old Town (great Mexican food), and an outdoor mall. I needed some civvies (civilian clothes) and I had money to burn—ten weeks of salary plus travel expenses. So the mall was really cool. Anyway, I went with some other guys from boot camp, but they were from the wrong crowd. I ended up having to find a way home because they got drunk at Sea World. The friends that I usually hung out with never left the base. They were anxious to go home in a few weeks and didn't want to get in trouble or bashed.

One day I wanted Mexican food so bad that I headed out alone to Old Town for chow. At the time, it was in a remote part of the city without a lot of local transportation. I had to walk all the way back to the base—several miles. While walking down the street, I saw lights coming down a hill toward me. My heart started pounding as a car slammed on its brakes in front of me. I dashed around it and jogged downhill as fast as I could. By the time I reached the bottom of the hill, the car was catching up to me. Out of nowhere, a Jeep Wrangler cut me off from the front. This was getting crazy. All I could think of was jumping down the hill into the bushes and making my way to the base that way. It was better than being bashed. Before I could jump into the bushes, I recognized someone in the back of the jeep. A young, crazy-acting guy was yelling my name. It was a friend from boot camp. By this time, the people from the first car jumped out to grab me. The Jeep unloaded three marines and a couple of navy guys. A third vehicle pulled up, a truck, with more marines and two navy SEALs. I looked up to heaven and said, "Thanks, Dad." In all my travels, I can really say that God has taken care of me. I love Him dearly.

Everything happened so quickly. All I remember was the threatening car leaving after a brief confrontation. Shore patrol (military police) eventually showed up, but they let us all go. My friend from boot camp was a brother to one of the SEALs and recognized me running down the hill. After that day, I decided to stay on base for a while. I eventually kept myself busy helping in the base chapel services. I sang with the choir (I sounded terrible), handed out programs, and assisted the chaplains. It gave me an opportunity to see how other church services were conducted. Volunteers helped with both the Catholic mass and the Protestant service each Sunday. It was different from boot camp services. Boot camp church was a few nice words about God, and then it turned into a pep rally. At this base, church was a place to meet with God and connect with Him. At every port or duty station I visited, I purposed to find a church to attend. No matter what part of the world I was in, Christians were my family. I believe that with my whole heart.

One day, during the time we were at training, each of us received what was called a "dream sheet." We were told to write down which bases, anywhere in the world, we wanted to be stationed at. I prayed for a second about what I should write. Everyone, of course, put his home city or state. I did too, but not for my first choice. I put Los Angeles as my first choice, Texas as second, and New York as third. Hey, I figured I was only in for two years so I might as well see a couple of places with good sight-seeing. Plus, we two-year-guys had already been informed that we wouldn't travel outside the continental United States. That ruled out Hawaii. Fortunately, I spent over three full months there on liberty over my stint.

Training ended and the fleet was my next destination. Everyone received duty orders based on those dream sheets. I was given my first choice—but didn't know it! I had to ask my instructor where this place—Long Beach—was.

I was instructed to report to USS Lewis B. Puller docked in Long Beach, California, on August 17, 1991, my birthday. Long Beach was just ten or twelve miles west of Los Angeles. I was excited about spending two years in the city I had always loved to visit as a child.

I grabbed my bags to pack and head out. When I was emptying my locker, a tall gentleman approached me and asked if the rack on top was taken. I told him, "Wise choice, because you could get peed on." I shared my story and we both laughed. His name was Robert, and I didn't know it then, but we would end up serving our entire enlistment together. He became a friend that I still talk with today, eleven years later.

I graduated from apprenticeship on August 1, 1991. I went home for fifteen days leave and then back to California.

6

REPORTING FOR DUTY

I caught the 8:00 P.M. flight out of Houston, Texas, to Long Beach, California. While I was sitting on the plane, I thought, "What a unique birthday present—to be reporting to my first command on my birthday. Is this preordained or what?" During the flight, I recalled that first night on the flight to boot camp when I missed the meal and slept instead. I thought about doing the same thing again. But wouldn't military life onboard be better than boot camp? I hoped so. I decided to eat the meal and nap afterward.

When I got to Long Beach, I was a little uncertain about what to do. I called the ship's phone number listed on my duty orders, but kept being routed back to the base operator. I explained to her that I was reporting to my ship, the Lewis B. Puller (FFG-23) for the first time. The operator told me that my ship was out to sea. Great. "For how long?" I asked. She didn't know for sure...or perhaps couldn't say. She recommended that I talk to the base duty station, and put me through to them.

The base duty-station clerk told me that they could send a shuttle to pick me up or I could wait for the bus coming by any hour. Either choice was an hour wait. I paid a super shuttle van to take me to the base duty station. Good thing I did. The base was only ten minutes down the street from LAX airport.

Super shuttles were a great way to get around. Five to eight people going in the same direction would fill a van and pay between

ten and twenty dollars apiece to share the ride to their destination.
I usually paid $10 whenever I flew in to Long Beach, or $15 coming
in from Los Angeles. I heard about the super shuttle from busi-
nessmen picking up their luggage at baggage claim. Cab fare could
cost $30 to $40 a person.

After arriving at the base duty station, the duty clerk told me
my ship would be back in a few days. He gave me a meal pass,
pointed to the galley, and assigned me a room to crash. These
rooms were similar to dorms with community showers down the
hall. As I was checking in, another sailor was also reporting to my
ship. He told me not to hang around the room in the morning to
avoid being put to work by the master-at-arms. He advised me to
dress in civilian clothes and enjoy the base. He recommended that
I stay on base rather than explore the city since this was my first
duty station. The base had a mall, Burger King, Taco Bell, and
a movie theater. I think he was concerned that if I went out by
myself, I might get lost or in trouble.

I went back to my dorm that first night and crashed until
breakfast. My new friend came by to make sure I knew the way
to the galley. The rest of the day, I spent exploring my new base.
The next night I was about to crash again when my door opened
suddenly. It was another sailor, who also had to wait for his ship.
Although my room was equipped to accommodate four people,
each with a rack and locker, my first thought was, "Hey, this is my
room dude." But after talking to him, I found out he was a believer.
We started talking about his walk with God, his church, and stories about his trips. It seemed as though he was pretty devoted to
God. He had some videos of sermons from his church back home
in the Philippines. My room had a TV and a VCR, so we watched
these sermons before going to bed. I was glad to have been able
to visit with another believer before going to the ship. I thought
about many things after that night. One of them was, would I be

the only believer on board? It was good to know that there were other Christians in the U.S. Navy.

The next night my ship came back to port. The other sailor was already waiting outside with his bags for the duty van. I was right behind him with my five huge bags on a pull cart. By the time I got to the end of the long walkway on the pier to our ship, the wheels came off the pull cart. I had stuffed everything I owned in those bags, at my mother's insistence. Nobody told me that I would only get a small locker to put everything I owned in, and military gear came first.

I was so embarrassed when I reported to the ship. I had no idea what to do, so I followed the lead of my friend. He asked for permission to come aboard after saluting the flag and was quickly accepted by the officer of the deck. The officer called down to the new man's department to report that he had arrived. Somebody showed up and took him right downstairs to the berthing compartment (sleeping quarters).

I was not accepted quickly. Not that they didn't care, or that they wanted to give me a hard time, but the ship had just returned from a three-week deployment. My department was the deck department, and this department was responsible for everything there was to do when the ship came into port. Our department was also the last to leave on liberty. We had to pull the ship to the pier using lines, tie up the ship, bird nests the lines, and then put rat guards on each line. There was no department phone to call, because our space was all over the place. So I waited.

Finally, the deck officer got a hold of a guy that was on duty who was part of my department. The officer of the deck was also in my department, but couldn't take me down below because he couldn't leave his duty station. I was about to follow the young man when I remembered about my bags out on the pier. I had left them all by the bow (bridge) so I didn't have to carry all of them.

He cracked up when he saw how much I had, and then lifted all my bags to carry them to the berthing compartment.

It was crazy down there. Everybody was taking showers, changing clothes, and running out the door for their liberty on shore. My guide just placed me in a corner and told me to claim a rack no one is using when the smoke clears. He also said to wait until chow time to ask for the duty master-at-arms to assign me a locker and to get my ship sticker. More waiting.

I sat and endured the obvious jokes about being a boot camp fish, fresh meat, and so on. I changed from my working whites (ice cream man suit) to my civvies. I headed to the mess hall and chowed with the duty section. One third of the ship's crew stood duty once every three days. Sometimes it was once every four or five days when we had enough manpower and nobody was on leave or TAD (temporary additional duty orders) for school. That night I met the master-at-arms. He gave me a locker and advised me that what wouldn't fit I could leave in the master-at-arms closet. The master-at-arms had a huge room full of handheld weapons and assault rifles. He also had a space used for storage for the crew. Since it was a weekend, I didn't have to do anything but hang out with the duty section.

Monday morning I met the entire deck department for the first time. It was like the first day of school for me. The department was full of misfits and slackers. Everybody in the deck department looked depressed. I found someone from Houston, Seaman Johnson. He and Seaman Hassler became my good friends almost immediately. These two guys didn't look depressed, but they didn't look like they were happy to be there either. That first week went so slowly. I couldn't imagine twenty-one months of this dull life. I had to find something to pass the time, even after work. I decided to pray, read my Bible, and fast whenever I had time. This was a practice that I would discipline myself into early on in the military.

I read fifteen chapters a day after work. I prayed for an hour or more lying down in my rack with my curtains closed and the light on. I fasted two to three times a week, every other week. I saturated myself in God's presence, building a strong devotional life during these hours of my nightly routine. Seeking God at that stage in my life built a spiritual foundation that stands today. I got used to praying in my rack over those years, and that's probably why I pray longer when I lie on my couch, floor, or bed rather than praying on my knees. After weeks of my doing this every day, the department started noticing. Even though I went to a movie or to the mall once a week or so, most of my time was spent reading and praying. Crewmembers had warned me that I would get three bad habits from the military: I would curse, smoke, and drink coffee, but I did none of these things during or after my time in the military. There's nothing wrong with coffee, by the way; I just don't like it. Never have.

I could tell that all eyes were on me because I stood for Jesus. My department heads were harder on me than on anyone else. They wanted to see me slip up so they could say I was a fake. My shipmates expected more out of me. At any job site, there will be those who will do the least amount of work possible, just to get through the day. We called this skating. This was going to be an interesting journey in faith and discipline for me. Most of the department guys that were supposed to be helping with the duties were skating or napping. I saw evidence, once again, that this was the route God had chosen for me in which to demonstrate His miracle-working power. This was His training ground for me to learn patience and self-control.

7

FIRST PORT VISIT

The base was one bridge away from Long Beach—about a five-minute bus ride. The base had bus stops on all three of its exits, so I could get to the city easily. I took the bus to Ocean Boulevard and walked two blocks to the nearest mall. Some of the best Chinese food in Los Angeles could be found there. It wasn't a big mall, but I couldn't buy much anyway because where would I put it? I spent most of my weekends seeing the sights of the city by transferring from one bus to another. On one of these typical weekends, I found a church that wasn't too far from a bus stop, and I decided to visit the Sunday service. The members of this church were extremely cordial. I met a family who opened their home to me. I returned nearly every weekend and became involved with the church activities, including helping with Sunday school youth. I only attended on Sundays because in the beginning of my navy life I stayed on base during the workweek.

In my first month on base in Long Beach, I made several friends outside of my department. One of them was Petty Officer Medrano from San Antonio, who worked in engineering. He and his family always invited me to visit their home at base housing. They always prepared delicious, home-cooked Tex-Mex food! The best fajitas this side of San Antonio. He became a close friend who was like a big brother on the ship. His also being from Texas was an added bonus!

Life in general on the ship was also getting better for me. A few more recruits were assigned to our department, which meant more help doing the work. One of these recruits was Robert, whom I met at the apprenticeship quarters just as I was leaving. He was the new guy, so they asked me to show him around the ship. I was also supposed to set a good example for him.

Our ship was small—less than two hundred and fifty sailors. We could carry four hundred or so if necessary. It hadn't been hard to learn my way around. Robert and I hit it off right away. He thanked me for telling him about the top rack at the apprenticeship. A "pee-pee man" had struck again. We had a good laugh about it. Because our ship was a designated training ship for the weekend warriors (reservists), we always had reservists with us, either on weekends or during their two-week training, all year round. A group was reporting for the upcoming duty to Canada, so we had to find him a rack quickly.

Since the trip to Canada would be my first trip out on this ship, I was nervous. The crew kept messing with us new guys about which sailor was going to get seasick first. My worries were all for nothing. The first cruise out was fabulous. The ship sounded so strong crashing through the waves. Out at sea, we stood watches: at the helm, which involved driving the ship; forward lookout, which was watching ahead of us and beside us for anything near the surface; and aft lookout, which was watching behind and for man overboard. If you fell off the ship, you had better hope aft lookout was not asleep, because most of the time he was.

My first watch was at the helm. Learning to drive a ship has no learning curve on a smaller vessel—the length of a football field. Anyone could tell when a rookie was learning the driving ropes. The ship rolls hard if you swing too fast side-to-side. The crew would be bounced around so much that they called upstairs asking for the helmsman's name. That would be me. I eventually got the hang of it. In fact, my job was at the helm during man overboard drills. That was when I got to open up the ship and make sharp turns, then stop on a dime. That was fun! Well, the first day was fun. But then came the second, the third, the fourth, and so on.

I learned our course wasn't directly to Canada. Whenever we went out, we always did maneuvers with other vessels at sea. After seven days we finally arrived in Vancouver, British Columbia, a province of Canada just north of the state of Washington. The captain gave us duty workdays only. That meant that if you didn't have to stand duty, you were off. My duty section was off for four days, so I decided to take in the sights.

Vancouver was absolutely beautiful. The food was excellent and the parliament building looked like a castle. I wanted to go up to the mountains and get pictures. A local told me that a train ride up to Nanaimo was the best way to see the beauty of Canada. (After I got out of the navy, I traveled to several other places in Canada doing ministry, and found it all beautiful.) I headed to the train station and purchased a ticket to Nanaimo. I had enough money to get me there and back, but had little for food or anything else.

The train ride was about an hour and a half. The only thing I hadn't checked was that the train only ran Monday through Saturday. I was arriving on the last train out of or in to Nanaimo. That meant spending a night somewhere until Monday night! The faith walk continued.

From the train station, I hiked to find some places to take pictures of the mountains and other scenery. I saw a soccer field when I was coming back down from the mountains. Several guys were playing a pickup game, so I went to check it out. They asked me to play, and of course, I did. We played three or four fun and energizing games. Afterward, I asked them if they knew of a cheap place where I could stay the night. I explained that I had come with little money and not expecting to stay the weekend. One of the players owned a motel around the corner. He said he would let me stay one night for $20. Praise God! God had provided for me that night. I would have $20 left for a meal in the morning and a bus ride back to the base. The guys dropped me off at the motel. After showing in my room, I went to get a burger. When I got back to my room, I rested and prayed.

After praying, I felt the Lord urging me to go to church the next morning. Opening the phone book in the motel room, I found a few churches. I went to the front desk to ask the clerk which church was closest. In the morning, I headed to the one he had indicated. I almost decided to sleep in, but I couldn't get away from that feeling of having to go. I had to carry my bag with me because I only had the room until noon.

The greeter at the door of the church was named Larry. He gave me a strong handshake, welcomed me to the service, and asked if I was visiting. My bag must have been a dead giveaway. I told him I was a sailor in the U.S. Navy. Since we were docked nearby, I had decided to visit these beautiful mountains. He invited me to his home for lunch or supper. (I forget what he called it.)

The service was great. God's presence was in that place. I also made another friend, Darren, while sitting in the pew. We talked before service about the military. He also asked if I had plans for dinner. I told him I was having a meal afterward with Larry, but that I could do dinner later. He was excited that I could join his family as well. Canadians are generally the friendliest people you will ever meet. Tell me of a church in America that you could go into and get two dinner invites by two complete strangers in under an hour.

After the service, I went with Larry to his house to have lunch. I told him and his family how I met the soccer players and was given a room for $20. They insisted that I stay the night in their guest room. The family then took me on a tour of Nanaimo, sharing its history and introducing me to a snack called biscotti (double-baked cookies). I loved it. The next morning after breakfast, Darren picked me up for another tour around the city. Later, he took me to a Wendy's fast food restaurant for lunch. The burgers tasted a little different than they do in the U.S. Canadians say they have better beef than the USA has. I disagree. Don't try to pass that over on a Texan. After lunch, we headed to the train station. Darren and his family had bought me a ticket already. That was great because I could only afford a bus ticket. Darren told me that he had to bless me because he knew I was God's servant. My time in Nanaimo eventually ended. Larry's family gave me a whole box of bisque for the road. This was my first port visit and God was already teaching me how to walk by faith. Literally!

I arrived back on the ship that Monday evening. Several hours later, we were underway, heading to Seattle for a day before returning to Long Beach.

8

FULL SPEED AHEAD, CHRISTIANS ABOARD

The deck department began the process of prepping the ship for dry dock. In dry dock, we would gut the ship inside and out. But before we went to dry dock, we had to take the ship out for some test runs. We would test all the systems by firing our missiles, torpedoes, and other arsenal. The ship would max out its speed and take hard turns. During one of these many test trials, I met a new friend.

Walking down one of the passageways near engineering, I heard someone singing. As I got closer to the sound, I recognized a verse of the song—"when praises go up blessings come down." I was surprised that he was singing so openly about the Lord. I stopped him in the passageway as he was passing me.

"Hey, I love that song!" I told him.

He grabbed me by the hands and yelled, "Then sing with me, son!"

He started singing again and pretended to punch me in the stomach. I smiled and sang along. Some of the crew passed us, looking at us as if we were crazy, but that day I found a friend who would encourage me to be bold in my faith. Ted Ward was his name; (I called him Teddy). He would continue to challenge me to be a man of God and never be ashamed of my faith. He helped guide me into boldness with the love and warmth of a friend. That night was a good night. Teddy was standing watch in engineering, watching the systems. I spent a few hours with him, talking about my walk with God. He shared how he had preached on television. He was a pastor and had a radio program.

Ward's influence started to rub off on me. One time when I was on forward lookout, I had to do the entire four hours topside. There were no rotations because the department was involved in getting the ship ready for dry dock. Whenever I stood on watch, I prayed aloud. Nobody could hear me, except for this one time, when the old man (the captain) heard me. He was outside smoking. He told the officer of the deck that I was talking to someone upstairs—which was a distraction I shouldn't have to deal with. The officer of the deck called me on the headset and asked me who was up there with me. I told him nobody. He got really mad and ordered me to his office.

When I got downstairs, he asked me in front of the captain, "Who were you talking to up there, Yanez?"

I looked at the captain and the officer and replied with conviction, "God."

They both stared at me with a surprised and puzzled reaction. When they saw I was serious, the officer asked sarcastically, "What were you talking to him about?" Everyone in the pilothouse started laughing. I stared straight into the eyes of the officer and replied with sincerity, "I asked Him to save you, each and every one of you." The loud laughter turned immediately into silence. The captain broke the silence by patting me on the back saying, "Padre, pray for all of us but not out loud during watch, okay?"

I gave the expected yes sir and headed back to watch. After that incident, the captain always called me Padre.

Another time Ward's influence encouraged me to be bold was on the mess deck. I was standing watch on forward lookout again, not excited to be there. I wasn't praying either, just leaning against the rail staring at the sunrise. I heard a whisper. I looked around me, but nobody was there. I heard it again. This time I said, "Lord I didn't hear you." Silence.

A minute or so later the voice returned and said, "Tell my people not to limit me." I thought on this for a minute. Then I said, "Lord how do we limit you?" Silence again.

Suddenly I heard a shout so loud in my ear that I had to take my headset off. The voice declared, "They limit me on how I answer them. They limit me on how I could heal them. They limit me on how they can come to me. They limit me on how I could help them. They limit me on their blessings. They limit me on the way they worship. On the way they praise. On the way they seek. On the way they teach. On whom I could save. They LIMIT ME."

I gripped the rail for support; my knees nearly buckled under me. Here in the middle of the ocean, God spoke to me so clearly.

"Who can I share your words with, Lord," I prayed. Silence.

Eventually I was relieved from the watch, so I headed to the mess decks for breakfast. I carried my tray to a table where my friend Teddy was eating with another Christian, Brother Robertson. My Catholic friend Scott saw me sit down and asked if he could join us. As Scott was sitting down, I told Teddy what happened on watch. He looked at me, smiling as usual and asked me why I was so down. He told me that I should be excited because God had spoken a word to me in the middle of the ocean. So I asked Teddy whom he thought I should share it with. The smile left his face as he looked at me with a disappointing stare. Then he pushed all of our trays aside and climbed on top of the table.

"Listen up, guys," Teddy yelled. God has spoken to Seaman Yanez. He told him to tell you people not to limit God. So don't limit Him. Hallelujah!"

Teddy motioned to me to join him on top of the table. I was too afraid that it wouldn't hold us both. Teddy was a pretty big guy. After Teddy said this, everyone stood quiet for a minute then began to eat again. God was using Teddy to charge my spirit and ignite more boldness in me. I would need that boldness to do what God had called me to do.

Shortly thereafter, I met another Christian who seemed to appear out of nowhere. His name was Ms1 Storm. He was a mess cook (chef) in the crew's galley. Storm and I became friends the last year I was on the boat. We would hang out together after work. All his family was in Washington State. So he hung out on the ship like I did during off duty hours.

Whenever I left the ship, I always spent too much money. The only time anyone could spend money on the ship was when he ordered a pizza. Pizza delivery guys ran back and forth to all the ships every night. You could talk them down on the price. Usually on base, a large pizza would cost $5-7. Anymore than that and you were being robbed. It was always good to have a mess cook on your side to get extra snacks and such.

One more Christian friend came in late into my tour. I think it was during our last visit to Hawaii when he came aboard. He kicked me out of my rack, a seniority thing. I got a lot of ribbing by the guys about that. It turned out he was a Christian and one of our department heads. His name was Bm1 Guilory. I called him Gil. One time he prayed with me in the bulldog room (our nickname for our conference room), and I truly felt the power of God. I mentioned Rm1 Robertson already. He was a radioman. Radiomen didn't actually listen to the radio. They were into communications, code talk, and that kind of secret stuff. Robertson believed in God and always talked about his faith. He was an inspiration in his knowledge of the Word of God. I mentioned Seaman Scott. He was a great friend. He was a devout Catholic and gave me insight into how he believed. He loved Jesus so much. We shared many things in common, like reading and praying. His devotion was amazing. He once wanted to convert me so he could get me canonized for the miracles God did on the ship. As you could see, I was not as alone as I first thought I would be. God placed me but among several brothers that were not ashamed of their faith. Each one of them was at a different spiritual level, and their beliefs varied. But these guys where the first ones I would go to for advice, for prayer, and for counsel when I was down. They were like brothers.

One time I was so frustrated that I didn't want to study after work. I decided I wasn't going to pray that night because I was tired. My heart had been tugging at me all day to spend a few minutes in prayer. I worked extra long hours that day, so I felt I could refuse to stay up to pray. I decided to ignore that tug in my heart and opted to hit my rack early instead. It was about two in the morning when I felt the Lord again calling me to pray. I decided to ignore the call in my spirit. Then I felt the call to pray again—even stronger. I finally said to God, "I am not getting up. I am tired and need my sleep. And there is nothing you can do about it." I was wrong.

In less than a minute, the lights came on in the berthing compartment. The rover on duty entered and began waking everybody. He said we had all been ordered to evacuate the ship. As I got to the pier, I noticed Teddy sitting in his pajamas on the curb. I walked over to him and sat down. I said, "Do you know why we had to get out off the ship?"

"Yes," he replied. "We got a bomb threat and had to evacuate."

I thought to myself, this is amazing. God called in a bomb threat to get me out of my rack. That taught me that if He wanted my attention, He could get it. After we returned to our racks later that night, I prayed for a few minutes. They were the most humble few minutes of my life. God is all-powerful. Amen.

9

FINDING FAMILY
AND FRIENDS
OUTSIDE THE BASE

After two months of talking about it, we finally made it to dry dock. The work wasn't as bad as I expected. We maneuvered the ship in a miniature dam-like cage and floated in it for a few days while divers worked underneath the ship to place the braces that would hold us up. When they were done, they drained the water out of the cage. The reason for the dry dock was to refurbish the ship, stem to stern, in five months. The job started by gutting out the insides of the ship. Since that meant tearing out our galley, berthing compartments, and work spaces, we needed a new home. That is where the floating barge hotel came into play. It had three different sections with three floors in each section. We had showers, galley, recreation rooms, and a few classrooms. We stood duty every five days or so, working until 3:00 P.M., then went home.

By the time we got in dry docks, I had already established myself as a minister on the ship. I started having a small Bible study in the evenings in one of the classrooms. We averaged about twelve people during the eighty sessions. My Christian friends that were on duty helped with the studies when they could.

We were in dry dock less than a month when the ship received devastating news. Our captain, who had been temporarily replaced so he could get well, had passed away the night before from a terminal illness. We hadn't had a captain since coming in to dry dock. Our temporary captain had sailed with us for a few months to get us to dry dock. It was so sad to see his family at this huge funeral filled with high-ranking dignitaries, military, and the press. He was a well-decorated captain and was loved by the men that served underneath him. The week after the funeral, we received a new permanent captain. We all nicknamed him Mad Max, because on his first day as captain he walked through the ship to inspect it. He found some metal and debris left from the welders and reacted angrily by throwing it over the side of the ship. He was angry that there was a mess all over the place. There were people welding at the bottom of the ship who barely missed being hit. He was a difficult captain to work under—rough around the edges and unapproachable. He made the officers on the ship nervous and had them running around in circles. Fortunately, most the crew had yet to encounter him.

While we were in dry dock, the holidays were quickly approaching and many of the sailors had gone on leave. Some were at schools or training. Others were serving aboard other ships. I hadn't saved enough money to make a trip to Texas for the holidays, so while others were on leave, I decided to visit some friends I had met over the past few months. I also contacted some of my extended family who lived in Southern California. I had seen them only once when I was little boy at my grandma's funeral. My Uncle Jessie was glad to hear from me and asked me over to his home for Thanksgiving. It was nice to have family to visit. Uncle Jessie (my dad's brother) is an amazingly nice and gentle man. He insisted on driving me back to the ship after visiting for the weekend. He didn't have to do that when I visited, but he did. God provided for me—a good man and an uncle—when I really needed one. His wife, my Aunt Sandy, was a sweetheart of a lady and a great cook. God also provided me with another necessary relationship in my cousin Julie. At first, she wasn't especially enthusiastic about hanging out with me. I think our first outing—inviting me to go along to the movies with Julie's friends—was her mom's idea. Maybe my "God thing" put her off. Anytime I talked about God, Julie would reply, "I see." But soon the awkwardness passed and we actually enjoyed doing things together. We both loved movies, loved to eat Chinese and Denny's, and we both loved to shop. I often took the bus from Long Beach and met her at the Cerritos Mall. We would hang out there for a while or head to another mall. Julie became my best friend. Since she had a car, we pretty much went everywhere together, unless she was working.

On those occasions, I took the bus to get around town. I couldn't go too far on the bus if I had to be back on base by the evening. The routes and times didn't always allow a return trip. In fact, I sometimes jumped on a bus or train just to see where it would take me and then go back the same way. One of those times, I took the train to Los Angeles from Long Beach and ended up in South Central. The train guy announced that we arrived in South Central then told me to get off. It was the last stop for the train. I walked down the street looking at all the crazy-eyed folks. They knew I wasn't from the area because I was carrying my usual department store shopping bags. No other trains were running, so I was stuck. The only thing I knew to do was jump on the next bus and ask the bus driver how to get back to my ship.

It seemed that my bus-by-faith approach to travel was a dud that night. The bus driver, Carol, told me how to get back to the base. But I had to get to the Cerritos Mall first. Her bus was going there, but probably would not arrive in time for the last connecting bus to Long Beach. During the bus ride, we talked about the Lord and the miracles He had done in our lives. She told me that I needed to meet her husband, Ron. He was also a minister, and she was sure he would enjoy spending time with me. Carol noticed the time was getting short to make that connection, so she called ahead on her radio to her base to see who was running the Long Beach from Cerritos Mall route. It was her friend Rhonda. She radioed Rhonda to see if she had a full bus. Rhonda told her that she was empty, and could give us about ten minutes to meet up with her.

We pulled up behind Rhonda's bus in the back of Cerritos Mall. Rhonda came out laughing and praising God. She announced loudly, "I hear we have a man of God to get back home to the base." I just smiled and greeted her. Just then, another bus pulled up behind Carol's. Out stepped another believer, Kenneth. He was finished with his route and heard the two women chattering on the radio, so decided to come and meet me. We had a good time for a few minutes until Rhonda had to leave. Just before I boarded her bus, Carol invited me for dinner on Friday to meet some more friends. I promised I would make it there if possible. God had been very gracious to me in all my bus-hopping experiences. Not all of them led me to relationships or divine appointments, but the ones that did I will never forget. There were plenty of other times I was so lost, that only by God's grace did I make it back to the base.

I met up with Carol and the gang on Friday to meet their friends and Carol's husband, Ron. We hit it off well together. He became a real good friend and influential minister in my life. He shared the Word of God so passionately and prayed with me whenever I visited. He gave me so much insight and perspective, but most of all, he was there for me when I needed him the most. I was a young man and needed guidance as to how to deal with the power of God in my life.

A young person who knows God talks to him becomes very bold. Others view this blessing as something close to obnoxious. They assume that you think you know everything. In addition, I had such a desire to share what God had said to me. I believed people would be awestruck and receptive to God's voice through me. But that never happened. I had to learn the reason I was given passion and visions that no one else saw or heard. The answer was simple, and my friend Ron helped me understand it. The vision was my burden to carry. Experience, patience, serving, and maturity will govern when I would see the dreams and desires come to reality. The Word of God gives several examples of young men with this burden. Take King David for instance. He was told as a boy to carry a burden of knowing he had God's favor. Not only that, but he also was told that one day he would be king. Imagine carrying that burden every day of your life. Look at Joseph's life for a moment. He was a young boy to whom God had given dreams and visions. He shared these visions with family whom he had trusted. Unfortunately, they were offended, jealous, and frustrated that he had so much favor with their own father and then even more with the Creator of the universe. One thing constant in the lives of David and Joseph is that they humbled themselves to God's will. Whether it was hiding in caves from a crazy king or being wrongly accused and locked in prison—they both just waited for their time to come in God's plan.

God placed special men of God in my life to mentor and instruct me. Ron was the type that would hear me out. Then he would tell me where I'd gone wrong or maybe needed some more understanding. Ron had a strong, authoritative voice, so when he talked people really listened. I had to practically force myself to receive their input in my life. I was naïve in my thinking that I knew the Word, knew about life and people, and that what I had learned in my upbringing was about all there was to know. But when I joined the navy and began meeting people with other backgrounds, different ideas, etc. I knew that I needed a firm, scriptural basis behind my thoughts and beliefs. I think the time in the navy made me research why, how, and what I believed in.

I thank God for putting these men of God in my life. When the Most High God speaks to a nineteen-year-old boy, listening to anyone else seems redundant and unnecessary. But a sign of maturity is waiting and not running. It took quite some time for me to learn the meaning of that simple sentence. I probably would have been less offensive or would have stepped on fewer toes if I just listened. If you want to be a great leader, you must observe all those who are around you. Include the good and the bad; observe their success and failures.

Maturity comes from knowing when and how to react to a circumstance. There were a couple of times that I restrained myself, and it paid off. When we lived on the barge, my rack was under one of our supervisors. He would make fun of me and fart at my rack. That wasn't that bad, unless I was in my rack when he farted. It got to the point that he would do that every night and every morning. He would say something like, "Wake up sunshine," and then he would fart on me. In the navy, a man's rank gave him some leeway, so I couldn't do anything about my supervisor's rudeness except place it in God's hands. I prayed one night that God would just deal with it, soon. That night as he slept, something happened to him. He was rushed to the hospital with dehydration. All I knew was when I woke up, he was gone. He didn't come back for three days. The day he came back to the barge, I was messing with my rack. I instantly got up from the floor so I wouldn't be farted on. He told me to hurry up and finish what I was doing, and he went to sit in the lounge. From then on, I didn't have problems with him. He didn't fart on me anymore and he was a lot nicer too. Hey, all you have to do is pray and sometimes wear a gas mask.

10

ALOHA, BABY.
I AM GOING TO HAWAII

Dry dock was finally over and amazingly, our next duty was to Hawaii. I was tired of being in dry dock and the prospects in Hawaii seemed more like a vacation than work. I told my friends from church that I was heading to Hawaii, and learned that one friend's grandparents were going to be in Hawaii around the same time. They gave me an address and number to get a hold of them when I was there. We didn't sail straight to Hawaii, of course. We spent about five days underway to get there.

The seawater in Hawaii was warm and clear. Most of the California waters were cold, and not too clear, but still nice. Hawaii was so much different, even though it is in the same Pacific Ocean. We had a swim call about five miles out from the beach. Swim call was when the crew could jump into the water and swim for a while. They would post gunners mates with rifles to be on shark look out. I swam for just a little while. Two guys with rifles covering my position was not too comforting. By the time they noticed a shark, I would have been eaten up already.

The first week we were stationed in Hawaii I stood on the base because we were in and out of the port every day. We participated in a REFTRA, which is refresher training and some war games. We did okay. We were sunk and had to cheat once to win. But those things happen. During the week, we spent four days,

Tuesday through Friday, out at sea for training and war games. On the weekends, we would be back in port.

On my first night out on the town, I left with a few friends to downtown Honolulu for some dinner. My friends were busy getting drunk in a bar while I walked up and down the streets checking out the shops. At one point, I noticed a man standing on a huge rock, yelling at the top of his lungs. After I got close enough to hear him, I realized he was preaching. He started asking if there was anyone who would stand with him. He kept praying aloud that someone would step up with him for Jesus. I don't know what happened, but I was being drawn to the rock. Then I started stepping up on to the rock. When I was about half way, the man on the rock pulled me up. He then gave me a kiss on the side of my cheek. He jumped off the rock and left me there, staring at people walking by.

I started to preach about God's love, then souls, and then God's miracle-working power. I held an altar call in the middle of downtown Honolulu. It was pretty awesome. I preached for about an hour. When I was done, I thought I was alone. But my friends came up behind me telling me they were ready to go back to the base. Toward the end of my sermons, my two friends had walked out of the bar. They saw me on the rock and sat down to listen. I told them I was surprised that they had waited for me. They replied that what I had preached about really hit them in their hearts. It was a quiet ride on the cab back to the ship.

We went out to sea for another four days, and when I got back, I called my friends from church in Long Beach to let them know I was in town. They hadn't arrived yet, but I talked to their daughter. She gave me the address of the church that her parents attended when they came to the island. I was able to get around town via cabs and bus rides pretty easily. I arrived at the church for a Friday night service. It was a small family church of about forty-five people. I met the pastor of the church; she was very nice. Her two sons, Leroy and Junior, helped build the church by preaching and leading worship. The church members were great to me. They took it upon themselves to show me around the best parts of the island. God had provided for me again. For the next three weeks, I called them every time I came into port and they were glad to pick me up and host me for the weekend. They always had a meal and a bed ready for me. They were great hosts.

During our sixth and last week in Hawaii, the captain gave us duty-only workdays. That meant that if you didn't have duty, you were off. I had ten days off in Hawaii! During the next ten days, I didn't even go back to the ship. Instead, I spent the entire time with my friends. I also preached at the church and visited as a guest minister at other churches. I enjoyed great food like chicken teriyaki, macaroni salad, and steamed sticky rice. I think it cost less than $4 per plate. On my last night on the island, the church had a cookout for me in my honor. At the end, one of the families drove me back to the base one last time. God provided for me an entire church that would become a fun, adopted family.

When I got back on the ship, my first lieutenant asked me where I had been for so long. I explained to him that since I didn't have duty for several days in a row, I spent my time off on the island, but I hadn't gone over a hundred miles from base. I then learned that even though we have liberty, we are supposed to call the ship to make sure our schedule hasn't changed or that our ship hadn't had an emergency. Oh well. They don't tell you this kind of stuff until you actually fail to do it. This is another military trademark.

We were then underway, en route back to our home port except for the training, which was for ten days at sea. It would normally take us only five days to get back to our homeport. So the rest of time, we drove around in circles around Catalina Island outside our homeport in Long Beach. Every time we had training, we would circle Catalina Island. Sometimes on watch, the quartermaster would chart out letters for our course. We would spell people's names in the water to fight off the boredom.

Occasionally men would respond to the boredom by getting testy. On one trip, I remember a new signalman came aboard. He was very demanding, not only to his department, but also to anyone he outranked. One day, I was on watch at the helm when he came up behind me and thwacked the back of my head with his finger. I yelled, of course, because it hurt, but also because the officer of the deck was standing beside me. The officer of the deck asked him what his problem was. He pointed to the message I had on my strap of my glasses. My regular glasses were broken, so I had taken a pair of these specially prescribed gas mask glasses and rigged them with a strap from some athletic safety glasses. The message I had written on the back of the strap said, "Jesus Loves You—Come Back to Him" in big bold black permanent marker. The signalman was angry that I was preaching to him through the message on the strap. He told the officer of the deck that I was violating his workspace. He requested that they send me downstairs to get some other glasses. I told him I didn't have any other glasses—that they were on order through sickbay.

That did it. The signalman went a bit crazy and refused to work. He grabbed me and tried to yank me off the helm. My good friend, Petty Officer Peake (one of my supervisors), was on watch in the pilothouse behind me. He grabbed the signalman and held him back so I could maintain the helm. Then he kind of giggled in his ear, telling him that he didn't want to touch the man of God, because then that meant he had to touch Him. Peake was my guardian angel on the ship. He was always there when I was in a tough situation. Once I asked him why he always took care of me. He said his momma would want him to.

The officer of the deck then intervened and asked the signal-man to calm down—that he was making a big deal over nothing. I interjected that it wasn't his fault, but was because of the conviction of the Spirit from the living God. That comment made the signalman freak.

Eventually, I was switched to aft lookout duty. That was cool with me. The signalman was just in a bad mood that day. Plus, aft lookout wasn't that bad during the day. The crew would hang-out on the fantail and talk to me. Sometimes they would bring me snacks or drinks. Time would pass the quickest back there. At night, some of the crew would come out to the fantail to stare at the seaweed, algae, and phosphorous that the ship's wake would break up. For a mile or so, we could see glowing debris floating behind the ship. Some of the crew were a little off mentally, claiming the water would talk to them. They insisted that the glowing debris was talking to them and telling them to jump in.

One night someone actually did jump. It was late one late evening and I had just finished my watch. I was ready to relax and read my Bible. I went to take a shower. Just as I started to lather up, I heard the bells and whistles go off for man overboard. The voice on the speaker said, "This is not a drill!" I was the designated man for the helm during man overboard, so I ran out of the shower, put on my green coveralls and headed to the pilothouse, still dripping wet with shampoo in my hair. The ship was swaying port to starboard at full speed, but I made it up the slippery ladders to the pilot-house to take the controls. When the officer of the deck saw how I looked, he refused to let me take the controls. I told him that I had been in the shower. Then the captain walked in and ordered him to let me on the helm. Hey, when the captain speaks you have to oblige. Finally, we got our guy out of the water. It turns out that our crewmember was a little over-stressed. He said the water had told him to jump in. This was a classic case of another sailor trying to get out of the navy. You wouldn't believe the things guys did to get out. Some would jump overboard, others knocked on the captains door naked, or said they were gay, and other dumb things such as getting popped on purpose doing drugs. Some people wanted out and wanted out now. Being away from family and friends was too much for some to bear. I think that some just didn't know what they signed up for.

We were out at sea for ten days straight after leaving Hawaii. Our ship was taking on fuel (refueling at sea) with a supply ship. That whole process takes a while. So you can imagine that when the captain told us that we were going to practice transferring supplies from ship to ship, we weren't excited at all. We were tired and ready for a shower. About seven of us, including Bm1 Guilory, were on the port side of the ship waiting for our turn for the supply drill. For some reason, Bm1 Guilory started singing, "He's got the whole world in His hands." Slowly all of us started to sing along with him. This was very interesting because I actually felt the presence of God touching me. Later on that night, Guilory told me he felt it too. These were the meanest and laziest guys in the department, yet for a few brief minutes, we had a glimpse into their hearts. They all genuinely loved and respected God. I found a thread of truth that ran through my entire time in the military: there is a mutual respect and love for God in almost every sailor, soldier, and pilot. We all knew that the jobs we did were dangerous. The only way that we saw the next day was by God's grace.

11

SOUND THE ALARM— MINISTER WENT AWOL

People deal with confrontation in different ways, but everybody has a choice as to how they react. Some react out of habit, others out of anger. Each response is your personal decision, whether it is conscious or subconscious. We are each responsible for our own actions. Sometimes when a person starts going the wrong way, he just keeps going, even when he knows it's wrong. That might happen because of fear—fear to return and face the hard issues. It could be that it's easier to be a good sinner than a bad saint. Sinning is easy, but living by God's grace is often difficult. God does make a way for all of us to escape temptation, but whatever damages we inflict on ourselves or others in the process have to be accounted for. God will give you grace to deal with the daily burden of your choices.

I know all of this by personal experience. I too did something stupid. I am not one of those ministers who tries to paint a beautiful picture of my life. I am telling you the truth about me, whether it's good or bad. I made and make mistakes just like everyone else. I know how it feels to disappoint friends, family, co-workers, and most important, God.

On September 1, 1992, I went AWOL (absent without leave) from my ship. It happened when we were in Hawaii a third time. I was preaching at churches and seeing the power of God move in people's lives. I started to question my effectiveness for God aboard the ship. After seeing God's power move in a church meeting, I soon found myself up back out to sea for maneuvers and standing watch. I made myself believe that the time for God's miracle-working power in my life was right then—but not while standing watch. We were scheduled to go out to sea for nineteen days en route to San Francisco. I decided that I was not going on that trip. I talked myself into believing that I was doing the Lord's will by leaving the navy. Even though the preaching was over in Hawaii, I felt I still had more preaching to do.

I was just seven months away from hearing the liberty call for the last time. What was I thinking? I sure didn't confide my plans to anyone. That should have been my first clue that I was not in God's will. I didn't want anyone to tell me I was wrong. Not that I would have listened anyway.

We had less than an hour before the ship went underway. I grabbed a bag of garbage and stuffed some clothes in the bottom of it. When I dropped the trash, I was supposed to grab my clothes out first, but my idea didn't work. The bag ripped while falling into the dumpster. My clothes ended up in the dumpster with all the garbage. I should have taken that as a sign to get my butt back on that ship.

One thing I did learn was not to jump ship without a major credit card. A small exchange was near the ship so I purchased some sandals, shorts, and shirts in there. I couldn't change on the base because my crew was still roaming around getting things ready for underway. In fact, I ran into my chief before I made it to the store. I told him I was going to get lemons for his lunch. Jumping into a nearby cab, I gave instructions to the cabby to head to the south gate. Ducking as we passed the gate sentry, my heart was beating so fast and I was scared. Anytime we have to sneak, hide, deceive, or lie, we should know automatically that we are outside God's will. I knew I was forcing something wrong into my life—pulling it in until I had what I rationalized was right for me. The outcome is always dissatisfying.

So there I was, running away from the ship. At first it was kind of exciting—the whole undercover thing. My first challenge was getting back to the mainland. The only place I could think of going for help was the YMCA. It was always available for military personnel around the country. I think it cost $10 a night. After getting to the YMCA, I drained my checking account with the ATM. I knew that my funds would post the next day or so from the direct deposit of my paycheck. I could only withdraw $300 a day, so I waited around three days to be able to collect $900. A mall was across the street from the YMCA and I bought some additional clothes, and then purchased an airline ticket to LAX. The only place I could hide out was at my Cousin Julie's apartment. I explained to her what I was AWOL. She just laughed at me thinking I was a crazy Jesus freak. She and I hung out for three days, and then she took me back to LAX so I could fly home to Houston.

Back in Houston, I preached at churches, schools, and on street corners. God's power was really moving. People were getting saved and healed. I was sure that I was doing what I was supposed to be doing. No, I was wrong to go AWOL, but it did show me that God can and will use a person for His purposes, even if he is outside His personal will. The Bible says that your gifts are not subject to repentance. God can use anyone to do His will. He used a donkey in the Old Testament to save a man from an angel by standing in front of them. He used a twenty-one-year-old who had jumped ship to preach the gospel.

I had planned a preaching trip to San Antonio, Austin, and Dallas, but I never made it to any of those cities. I had been gone twenty-eight days from my ship. The Holy Spirit started talking to my heart. Although His power was evident in my ministry, the

time was not His time. It was not the will of God for me to go
AWOL. That decision was one made by my immaturity and lack
of patience to wait on His will. My heart told me that my place
was back on the ship. I bought my ticket to return the next night.

When I got into my connecting city, Las Vegas, I called my
good friend and shipmate, Robert. It was about twelve at night, so
I apologized for waking him up. He said that he was just glad to
hear that I was alive and that everybody thought I had been kid-
napped or was dead. My operations officer, Lt. Nupher, was very
concerned about me missing. He had ordered a complete search of
the ship. Every compartment opened and every area searched. He
ordered them to break my lock to my locker and rack. When he
saw that my Bible was still in my rack and my ID, he thought the
worse. He actually yelled, "He left his Bible. Oh my God, something happened to him. He would never leave his Bible."

It was actually my spare Bible. I left it on purpose along with
and an extra ID to throw them off track. That way, they would
think I was still on the ship. I thought that would give me enough
time to get off the base. Sometimes even Christians can think of
the most devious schemes. We were only allowed one ID in pos-
session. Months prior to my going AWOL, I was tired of seeing
my old boot camp picture on my ID. I told them I misplaced it so I
could get another one. You can't get on or off your ship without an
ID. You also can't get on the base without one.

Lt. Nupher was a great guy. I felt bad that I disappointed him.
He even requested permission from the captain to stay behind to
search for me in Hawaii, but he was ordered to go with the ship.
After speaking to Robert, I knew I had to get back to the base. But
it wasn't until then that I realized the severity of my disobedience. I
started feeling the pressure not to return. Running away was on my
mind again. At that moment, I remembered a sermon I heard on a
Christian television station. A very popular minister was preaching

about running from your problems using a passage from Psalm 55:6. David said in the verse, "*Oh that I had wings like a dove! for then would I fly away, and be at rest.*" The TV preacher went on to illustrate that David wanted to just get away from his problems. If he were able to fly just anywhere in the world to get away, he would have. But flying away would not have provided an escape. He couldn't leave his problems behind, because his problems were internal, within him. No matter where he went, they would be waiting there for him. Eventually these problems would overtake him, dragging him back into the same scenarios of disappointment. I knew if I didn't stop right then and turn myself in to the military, I would be in deeper trouble. It was me, not sin or some other outside influence, and I had to stop running from these problems. Fear was holding me back. My flight was being called over the public address system. I heard a faint voice saying "last boarding call for Los Angeles." Looking at my ticket, I prayed to God, telling him I trusted Him even though I had messed up. I knew He would give me grace and mercy. I trusted Him. Turning around, I boarded the plane to Los Angeles.

I arrived in the middle of the night. I had made arrangements with my cousin Julie to stay at her place. Julie was surprised I was still out AWOL. I think she actually was starting to worry that I was taking this too far. She voiced her concern by saying to me, "You're still on that thing?" She had a bed made for me on the couch when I arrived. It was pretty late, so we didn't have time to talk much but she seemed very quite. In the morning, I took a bus back to the base. When I showed my ID to the base guard, my heart started pounding. In my mind, I thought everyone was still looking for me. As I waited for the base transport bus, I thought about changing my mind.

From across the way I heard a familiar voice yelling, "Yanez!" I looked around and saw Petty Officer Peake honking the horn of his friend's car. "Yanez! I thought you'd never be back!"

God's timing is breathtaking. Peake arrived at the precise moment of my desire to flee once again. Do you realize the size of the base and the probability of my sitting in that spot at that precise moment of Peake driving by? He looked at me and could tell I was scared. "Hey, you're not going anywhere, son," Peake said. "You need to turn yourself in. You'll be alright." He made his friend get out of the driver's seat (it only had two seats) and wait for the bus. He then took me in his friend's car back to the ship. That was another divine appointment. Normally, our ship moored at Pier 19. That week the ship was moored at Pier 15. I would have had to look all around for the ship. Instead, Peake drove me straight there.

When I approached the ship, I kind of just froze. I prayed silently to God, asking Him for just a little help. The answer was immediate. Peake put his hand out to me and said, "We'll do this together." Grabbing his hand, I walked up the brow to the ship's quarterdeck and requested permission to come aboard. The officer of the deck took my ID and immediately called the master-at-arms.

Then it began. Crewmembers came from all parts of the ship to stare at me. The master-at-arms asked, "Is this your only ID, Yanez?" I said that he knew I had another ID in my rack. They were about to take me below deck when Lt. Nupher stopped them. He pulled me aside, asking me to follow him. We walked to the fantail. He told me he was disappointed in me, that he thought we were good friends.

Lt. Nupher truly was a nice guy. He always treated me right. For example, a few months before I went AWOL, I was supposed to report for duty down to the mess decks. Instead, he made me his yeomen (personal secretary) for a month or so. He was third in command of the ship, so there some benefits to working for him.

Back to the fantail discussion. Lt. Nupher told me that he would not be able to protect me. Neither could he pull any strings for me, because that wouldn't be fair.

I decided that the truth was my best defense. First, I apologized to him as a friend. Second, I admitted that what I had done was foolish and irresponsible. No one was to blame but myself and that's why I had come back to pay my dues and finish my tour.

Nupher actually had a tear in his eye. He told me four other guys had gone AWOL at the same time in Hawaii, and that the captain was going to deal harshly with all of them. He said we were going to be made examples of to the fleet. Since I had been gone the longest, I would probably get the worst punishment. That didn't make me feel any better.

After speaking with Nupher, I went down to the berthing compartment to find a place to hide. My department was waiting for me. Most of them laughed and joked about the situation. It was all okay, that didn't bother me personally. But I was bothered that I had left a door open for ridicule—the door that led to my work in faith with this crew. I could take all the jokes about my situation, but jokes about God, Jesus, the Holy Spirit, or the faith that I believed in were shameful. That brought me down, but I had no one to blame but myself.

It was a grueling first day back on the ship. I was summoned to the chief's mess. Since we didn't have a JAG (judge advocate general) on the ship, I was assigned a chief petty officer to represent me. "Great," I thought, "now I won't even get fair representation." I was given the option of taking my case to the local base JAG, but decided that I would rather be judged by my peers. I then had to write my side of the story from beginning to end. They gave me one sheet of paper. I used the front, the back, and three more sheets of paper. When I turned it in, the chiefs broke out laughing, asking if it was the new gospel according to David. From there I reported to the master-at-arms locker. All my gear was stored there after they busted the lock on my rack. Everything seemed to be accounted for, so I signed the release log and took my things back to my berthing compartment. I had to settle for a top rack. That wasn't so bad, but I didn't get a coffin locker.

After I found my rack, I was summoned to admin and disbursement. I threw my gear up into my rack, because I had no time to unpack. Admin had me fill out paperwork needed for my personal file. Disbursement let me know I couldn't be paid until captain's mast was complete. I was broke, but it didn't matter because I was restricted to the ship. There was no place to spend money except the ship's store.

The next few days were difficult for me, so I didn't eat. Not because I was fasting or praying, but because I really didn't want to see anyone at chow. Even though I was waiting on the captain's mast, I still had a workday with my department and extra duty until 2030 (8:30 P.M.) every night. During one workday, I was walking by the passageway outside engineering. Teddy was coming out of his department and saw me. I was so ashamed; I couldn't even look at him.

Teddy put his arms around me gently saying, "My brother has come back to me." He told me that I had been struggling, but now I was back. Not to worry, God would take care of me. He gave me a huge hug and reassured me that everyone has his or her own valleys to walk through. He also told me that he had been praying for me and that God had already told him that I was coming back. Ms1 Storm later shared the same words of encouragement. Eventually, the rest of the Christian brothers aboard all comforted me. Now all I had to do is wait for captain's mast and see if I still would be in the military.

During the interviews by the chief, I was read the three charges against me. One was missing ships movement in Hawaii. Two was missing ship's movement in Seattle. Three was absent without leave for twenty-eight days. They dropped a fourth charge, which was another missing ship's movement in San Diego. Missing ships movement three times meant an automatic dishonorable discharge and possible prison time. So Lt. Nupher was able to convince them to drop one missing ship's movement charge. That was good, because that would have sunk me for sure. After the second day, they gave me a time for captain's mast—Friday, before we went underway for three weeks. So that gave me a little bit of closure. By Friday, I would know my destiny—whether it would be me finishing my enlistment after serving my punishment or the big chicken dinner—a dishonorable discharge from the military with maybe some time to serve. I set myself up in my rack as I usually did, ready to meditate in the Word and pray to God. It's hard to hear God or even feel His presence when you are feeling shame and disappointment. Pressing in, I reached for Him. I felt nothing. But I kept on reaching. Loving God is all I knew.

12

CAPTAIN'S MAST AND THE SENTENCING OF THE REV

Friday seemed like it took forever to arrive. Perhaps it's that was for all guilty men. Around 1600 hours (4:00 P.M.), I was told to appear in dress white uniform for captain's mast. After getting dressed, I went to the port side of the pilothouse near the flag station. That is where the other four guys that went U/A (unauthorized absent) were waiting. We had a few minutes to talk before lining up to go in, one by one, to see the captain and our peers. The other guys surprised me by asking me to pray for them.

"Are you sure?" I asked.

The guys told me that I was still "the rev" to them. They felt my situation was different, because I had spent my time away doing good—saving souls and helping people. They had spent their time drinking and partying. Before I knew it, I was praying for each of their requests. I asked each one of them what they wanted out of this captain's mast. Some said they wanted to go home—they wanted a discharge from the navy. The others wanted to finish their tour. No one wanted judicial punishment. Just after I finished praying for those guys, the master-at-arms came out.

"Line up!" he instructed.

One by one, the other men entered the pilothouse. After a few minutes, we could hear "Mad Max" yelling. When each had finished, he came back to shake my hand and tell me that he had gotten the decision he wanted. Those encouraging outcomes gave me that little bit of holding on that I needed before I entered for my turn.

My case was the last one to go before the captain. As I entered the pilothouse, I saw that every chief on the ship was present for these proceedings. That's about twenty chiefs, senior chiefs, and master chiefs, all together, standing by the instrument panels. My immediate thought was that I was done for sure. These were the same chiefs who were cracking up and making fun of me for my long letter of explanation down in the chief's mess. The officers of the ship stood on the other side of the pilothouse. There were about sixteen of them—all but Lt. Nupher who was absent. The captain stood straight in front of me behind a lectern in between the Navy flag and United States flag. Standing at attention, I requested permission to enter. The captain granted me permission. That was a very hard first step to take. At that moment, however, I sensed a comfort in my spirit. All my anxiety lifted. In fact, I had to fight with myself not to giggle or smile during my captain's mast. Stepping into the pilothouse, I marched forward until I was directly in front of the captain. Still standing at attention, again I saluted him.

"At ease, Yanez. The charges against you are very serious. I have thought long and hard about your letter of explanation. Frankly, I was impressed that not once did you claim that God was your excuse for leaving the ship. I was also pleased to read that you want to stay in the navy until the end of your tour."

The captain paused for a moment to find something on the lectern. He picked up his reading glasses. "Here are the charges against you, Yanez—"

"Wait one minute!" Lt. Nupher burst into the pilot house, interrupting the captain. "I am dismissing his counsel. I wish to represent Yanez."

The captain didn't look pleased. "I told you to stay downstairs," he said. "You're not going to stop these proceedings. Step outside with me, lieutenant."

The captain and Nupher talked for a few minutes privately in the outside of the pilothouse. When they returned, Nupher stood beside the officers while the captain went back to the lectern and continued.

"Originally, I had planned to rule on this case myself," he said. "But I have decided to allow all of your peers to weigh in on your verdict."

The captain turned over the floor to any chief or officer that had an interest in speaking on my behalf. To my surprise, the admin chief stepped forward. "Yanez is a good guy and a good sailor. It would be a mistake to let him go."

That short remark started an avalanche. Every chief and every officer had something good to say about me. The mess chief said I was an encouragement to the mess decks. He would give me the hardest jobs all the time to try to break me. He said I never complained but did the jobs and usually sung a hymn. His recommendation was for me to stay aboard. Another chief mentioned that my faith was an inspiration and that I had learned a valuable lesson about faith and responsibility. He too suggested that I stay on board to finish my tour. The master chief really battled for me and so did the senior chief. They both recommended that I stay aboard the ship. Even the chiefs from engineering, whom I had never worked with, knew who I was and about my work performance. They had all stood duty with me at one time or another. They asked that I stay aboard. Even the chiefs that shared the master-at-arms responsibilities had a good thing to say about me. Then there was the biggest shock of all. The chief of my department stated that I was one of his hardest workers. That everyone in the department drew from the wealth of my faith and compassion.

He recommended that I stay in his department to finish my tour. After all the chiefs had finished their recommendations, the officers continued by backing up their recommendations. And of course, Lt. Nupher's testimony went on and on for me. I stood speechless.

God used my peers, including some I barely knew, to imprint a message that would never leave me. No matter what you do or where you're at in life, everyone can see who you are by the way you live and work. So live every minute of your life for God.

After everyone had spoken, the captain looked at me and told me to stand at attention. "Yanez," he said. "I hope you realize what happened here today for you. These men, your peers, came out on your behalf of their own volition. No one asked them to defend you. Your shipmates care about you. You're obviously important to the morale of this ship. You're important to the crew because of your faith and compassion. In my thirty-two years in the navy, I have never seen a ship respond to one of their shipmates like this before. Yes, it was stupid for you to walk away from your duties, to miss ship's movement twice, and to be gone for twenty-eight days. But the biggest disappointment was letting all these men down. Nevertheless, they sound like they still believe in you. In fact, I still believe you. Don't make this mistake again."

"Yes, sir," I replied.

Then the captain asked, "What sentencing do you think would be proper for these charges."

"Three days bread and water, sir." That would be a severe punishment from the navy's perspective.

The captain started laughing, then replied, "Padre." (He called me padre because I was a preacher. The amazing thing was that God gave me extreme favor with him even though he scared everyone else.) "I know that you could fast that in a heartbeat. Nice try."

He continued, "Forty-five days restricted to the ship and forty-five days extra duty; one-half month forfeiture of pay for two months and reduction in rate. This captain's mast is adjourned."

That was it. I don't know who was happier, Lt. Nupher or me. He was hugging everybody and shaking hands as everyone left. After I was officially dismissed, he gave me a big hug and told me I was going to be okay because he had just arranged for an extended testing exercise. For the next six weeks, we would be out in the water and we would only come back to port a couple of times for a few days. It was almost as if everyone was serving the restriction with me. Underway there wasn't any extra duty because we stood watches. So it all worked out. I would be able to finish my tour.

When I got back to my berthing compartments, all the guys in my department gave me hugs and shook my hand. Serving the restriction was easier than the extra duty. The days in port were the longest, mainly because I had to work until 2030 every night. My chief used that to his advantage by making me paint the sides of the ship every day for my extra duty.

Halfway through the restriction, I became really bored with everything about the ship. No McDonald's. No Burger King. We were cut off from the outside world. My friends in the supply department let me use the phone for a few minutes everyday when we were in port. I would call my friends at Calvary Assembly in Stanton, which I had attended many times during the past year. I had several new friends there like Pastor Don Wagner and his wife Georgia, Nathaniel Williams a great young man that plays music and sings, Shane Sowers, a young minister, and of course the youth group and senior pastor. There I also had met a special family that adopted me. We called them the Duran Clan. Mike and Gina Duran were the best of friends and family to me. They opened their home to me and treated me like a little brother. One time I went on a seven day fast—drinking only water. I went to

Mike and Gina's home at the end of the fast. I was very hungry. I went grocery shopping on the way there and after arriving, made a feast for everyone. Here is a quick tip: never go grocery shopping after a fast until you eat. You will buy everything in sight, eat it all, and eventually become sick. I made such a mess in their kitchen. But as I said, they were best of friends. Gina just threw her pans away and Mike said, "It's all right." Tell me how many friends would let you make a mess out of their kitchen and not freak. My friends at Calvary Assembly were glad to hear from me and to know that I was okay. I also called home and my cousin Julie to check in and see how things were going. Back then, the navy did not have telephones or internet for the public as they do now. We were out to sea, which meant we were out to sea. I think it's good that they have all that stuff now. It must make it seem like a job and not a prison for six months being out to sea. I went into a week-long depression. Nothing was helping me get out of this. I tried everything prayer, studying, fasting, and praising. But I still felt the same. At the end of that week, I went to lunch early. I was the first guy in line waiting for the door to open. I just wanted to eat lunch quickly so I could get at least forty-five minutes for prayer. I heard someone singing in the back of the line. It was Teddy. He was singing an old song that was one of my favorites. It was called "Praise the Lord." When he got to the part of the song that said, "...the chains that seem to bind you just fall powerless behind you. Simply praise Him," Teddy yelled out to me, "Yanez! Do you know He loves you? Brother Yanez. Do you know He loves you?" I didn't want to look back. Teddy kept crying out. I kept ignoring him. But then I heard Teddy whisper, "God just wants you to know that He still lives." After hearing that, I finally broke down. Slowly I turned my head looking pass the rest of the crew in line. The power of God fell on me in that chow line. Tears started pouring out uncontrollably. The line kept moving past me slowly.

I yelled out, "Brother Teddy! Yes I know he loves me!" Teddy cut through the line to catch up with me. He told me that it was important to know that I was forgiven and that God loved me the same. I cried, cried, and cried. God used Teddy to help me realize that I had to forgive myself. Everyone else had forgiven me: the crew, the navy, the captain, and my friends. But I hadn't. Those tears ended up being tears of joy. That day I forgave myself. It was not by my actions to enter to throne room of God; it was by His grace, which was Jesus Christ. I was forgiven because of the blood. Another friend of mine, Ron, told me to hold my head up. He told me that though a man falls, the Lord upholds him with His hands. He said we are to pick ourselves up. Dust ourselves off. And walk for the Lord. After that day, I knew I would be okay. By the time I was at the end of my sentence, I was feeling better. On one of the last extra duty days, I had to paint the passageway outside of our berthing compartment. I borrowed my friend's boom box and put on a Christian tape with worship music. The captain was walking around and heard the music. He called my duty officer over, who happened to be Bm1 Guilory. He told him to have me lower the music. So I did and kept on painting. Then the captain pointed toward me, telling Guilory, he was amazed at my desire to serve God. He also shared that one day when I will be preaching in a tent, he will walk in and give his life to Jesus, but not until then. Guilory just agreed with him, and then the captain headed back up to his stateroom. Later, Guilory told me to go buy a tent so we could save the captain. That is still my prayer today. Whenever I preach under a tent, I think of the captain. I always ask myself, is this that day? And I know one day it will be that day.

13

ROBBED AT SEA

I was on the last five months of my tour with the navy. We had just arrived back at our base in Long Beach from a week or so underway. I didn't have any special plans, so I went to the pier to use the phone booth there to make some phone calls. I was going to call some of my friends from the church in Stanton, California, and I also needed to check in at home to see how things were going. My friend was on pier watch, so I waved as I was passing. About two steps before I made it to the phone booth God whispered to me audibly. He said, "Your credit card is gone. It has been stolen."

Immediately, I asked the Lord, "Who took it?" And God told me the name of the person who had taken it from my wallet. It was weird. Why would God tell me that my credit card was gone? I made the call to my dad to catch up with him. While we were talking, I thumbed through my wallet, checking all my credit cards. After a minute or so, I froze for a second. My main credit card was not in my wallet. At that instant, I told my dad what God had just told me. He said to listen to God no matter how crazy it seemed. Quickly I hung up the phone to go back to the ship. Before I went back, I told my friend at the pier watch what God had told me. He knew I was serious and told me that he would call the ship if he saw the person whom I believed had taken my credit card.

When I got back to the ship, I searched my rack, lockers, and all my clothing. I found nothing. The Spirit had to lead me to find some kind of evidence before I told the master-at-arms. The only thing I could think of was calling my credit card company and going over the last few weeks' charges. I went to the admin department to use the phones there. I needed a desk to write on to itemize everything. My friend Scott was glad to help me. The credit card company told me $1,360 in charges had been made in the past week. Most of the purchases were from a country-style clothing store. I told the credit card company that was impossible because I had been out to sea. Plus, even though I am from Texas, I don't own boots or a ten-gallon hat. It seemed to me that a certain somebody had gone on a shopping spree. I asked the quarterdeck to call the master-at-arms for me. From the quarterdeck, I called the pier watch to let him know I had confirmed my card had been stolen, and it was likely by the person we suspected. The master-at-arms told me to meet him down at the chief's mess. After explaining to him that my credit card was missing, and whom I believed had taken it, his eyes lit up. Everyone apparently hated this suspect. This ship was waiting for something big to happen so that they could give him a major punishment. The master-at-arms told me to fill out a statement so he could start an investigation.

While I was on the mess decks filling out the statement, the pier watch called me at the quarterdeck. I ran upstairs to answer the phone. The pier watch told me that the suspect had just passed him on the pier and was on his way to the ship. I called the master-at-arms in the chief's mess to let him know I was going to confront the suspect. He told me not to do that.

The suspect came on the ship a few minutes later. I asked him if we could talk in the hanger, and he agreed. When we talked in the hanger, I told him that I couldn't find my credit card. I wanted to give him a chance just to turn it in. He acted surprised, and at first he was speechless. Then he offered to help me look for it, and suggested that maybe I had lent it to someone. I left it alone, but I knew he was lying. The suspect then went down to the phone booth to make a call. When he came back to the ship, the master-at-arms was waiting. They took him down to the lockers to search his gear. They didn't find my credit card, but they did find some other gear belonging to other crew members—some working pants and steel-toed boots. That was enough for the master-at-arms to take his ID and hold him on ship for investigation. The only thing I had linking him to my credit card were the purchases made at the stores he had shopped in. But I know what God had told me. I prayed that God would be clear in how I should handle this situation.

A few days went by and my statement came showing the unauthorized charges. I highlighted the dates and matched them with the ships schedule. The charges occurred only on the days we were out to sea. Then I remembered that when we went through the suspect's lockers, some new pants had been in there. I asked the master-at-arms if I could see the gear that was confiscated. Taking the billing statement, I matched three pairs of pants that had store tags still on them. The item numbers matched the billing statement. That was enough evidence for the master-at-arms to charge the suspect. I was relieved that was over.

Everybody on board was excited that we finally caught him on something. People were patting me on my back saying that it took The Rev to put the crook away. Everybody seemed a little too happy. That bothered me for some reason. I went to our lounge to watch TV. While I was sitting there, I felt a very strong impression to find the suspect. I had been told not to talk to him anymore, because it was becoming a serious federal investigation. This ship wanted this guy out and wanted him out now.

One of my friends was on watch at the quarterdeck. I called him to find out where the suspect had extra duty. They told me he was in the forward machinery room. It was a noisy space with very narrow aisles. When I got downstairs, I talked to the suspect. I told him my whole story and how God had told me what he had done. He started to cry. He said he was sorry. In fact, he repented and said the sinner's prayer with me. He told me he didn't want to go to jail. When we finished talking, I promised him that things would work out, but he had to trust God. He needed to be honest when questions were asked about the stolen card. He told me his wife destroyed the card, but he would pay all the money back. I didn't know if that would help because I had already reported it stolen. I was in a strange predicament. All my shipmates wanted to destroy this guy's life. On the other hand, I had a guy who was so scared, yet did this to himself. I prayed. Sometimes there's nothing else to do but pray.

The next morning the suspect brought me back every penny that he owed me. So I called the credit card company to tell them I was going to pay those charges, but to send me another card. I deposited the money and sent the payment. The credit card company notified the ship that there was no longer an investigation because the cardholder had accepted the charges and paid them. At that instant, everything changed. Since I wasn't going to prosecute, the entire ship turned against me! I have always said that a person's true colors will come out when he has no control of circumstances and everything begins to go south. Some of the crew even threatened me. I was told that if I didn't prosecute they would throw the guy overboard on our next underway. Some threatened to beat him or me if that's what it would take. We were scheduled to go underway that next afternoon.

The acting JAG officer told me that the military could still prosecute him without my testimony. This was a surprise to me. In fact, I was about to get a bigger surprise. The JAG officer told me that I would be held responsible for not testifying, and I could share the same punishment as the accused by not testifying. At first, I thought it was a scare tactic until I found out in the Uniformed Code of Military Justice that it was true. I spent that evening looking over UCMJ law books. Unfortunately, I couldn't find anything to help me make a decision. This left me in a dilemma. Testifying would secure his conviction because of the other two charges of stealing boots and a pair of pants. Not testifying would get me in trouble. Then there were the threats of harming us both and even throwing him overboard.

The next morning we were preparing to head back to sea. By this time, the entire crew knew what the acting JAG officer had shared with me. The best thing I could think of doing for both the accused and myself was pray. This took some faith and blind trust. Not only were my last few months in the navy at stake, but also another man's entire future. Before we went out to sea, my department heads told me that I needed to testify. They said the accused was in grave danger of being killed—murdered really—during the night by being thrown overboard or beaten to death. Rumors of a plan to harm the accused were flying all over. If I wrote a testimony down on paper, they could leave him ashore to be held in the base's brig until captain's mast. Again, I thought this was another attempt to coerce me to testify.

I chose to ignore their advice. The ship headed out. That day they sent me to forward lookout until the evening. I think this was punishment for not taking their advice. I was on watch in the same position in the rain for eight hours. Finally, I was relieved from the watch. That night I didn't get any sleep. Instead, I prayed the entire night for protection for the accused and myself. The morning came with another long day of the crew giving me the cold shoulder. Even through the mess line, I was told that I had better testify or they would poison him. I cracked up because it seemed like they were joking. They weren't.

About an hour before captain's mast, I went to the berthing compartment to get in my dress whites. As soon as I got to my locker, I was pushed against it by another crewmember. He started yelling at me that I had better do the right thing. Then a good friend of mine quickly pulled him off me. My friend told him that he didn't agree with my not testifying, but not to hurt me. About that time, two engineers came rushing in to threaten me by pushing me on the floor. I started to push them back so I could get up but they held me to the ground. About that time, Peake walked in from the lounge. He went crazy slamming them against a locker and holding them there. Then the rest of my department came out pushing people back so I could get up. It was nearly a riot! As soon as I got up, somebody pulled me into the rumble again. During this entire ordeal, I could not bring myself to retaliate. It was almost as if God held me back. I was gentle and meek—not even fazed by the hitting or pushing.

I was at the bottom of the pile. All I could see were bodies flying all over the place. Everyone who was helping me was already wrestling or punching someone. Then out of nowhere, a first-class petty officer jumped out of his rack. I didn't know him too well, but he worked in the same operations division.

"Stop it! Stop it!" he yelled. "Leave him alone!"

Amazingly, the fighting stopped. The petty officer continued.

"Why are we persecuting Yanez? Why? Is it because he is doing something wrong? Why is it wrong to forgive?" He started weeping. "He is only doing what Jesus told him to do. Forgive."

He grabbed me and started hugging me. "He is being like Jesus," he said. "He is standing on this ship showing us how to be like Jesus. He has forgiven, just like we need to do." He finished by saying, "We all know what is right, but we do not do it. Our mamas and grannies showed us, but we have ignored it. This is happening to remind us of what we are to do. Forgive because Jesus forgave us." He hugged me again and went back to his rack to cry.

Every man hung his head and left the room without a sound. The master-at-arms finally showed up to tell me I needed to go upstairs. My dress whites were a mess. Since I was only a witness, I could go to captain's mast with my inspection dungarees. I changed and headed up the ladders to the third level for captain's mast in the pilothouse.

The accused stood at attention in front of the captain, just as I had several months prior. I could relate to the stress he had to be feeling. They went over all three charges against him, one by one. Then they asked for a testimony from each witness. Since there were three charges, there were three witnesses. The guy with stolen pants testified, "I think this person should be given the worst punishment available. He stole from me and from my family. He is a thief and should be treated like one." The guy with the stolen boots testified, "I agree with the previous testimony. But I add that it is a serious sin to steal in my Muslim faith. This is an extremely punishable crime. I feel all resources must be used to make sure that this person serves as an example aboard the ship." When the captain learned I didn't want to testify, he gave me a way out. He knew the riotousness of the crew. He also genuinely cared about my situation. He told me the consequences of my not testifying, and then he asked, "To the best of your knowledge, was your credit card misplaced, stolen, or removed from your rack without your knowledge." Before I could answer, he warned me not to put myself in position to lie.

I answered the question truthfully. "Yes," I replied.

Before I could interject a defense for the accused, he shut me down by ordering me not to speak. I stood there until they found him guilty of all charges. Then the captain gave me the chance to speak on sentencing, but only if I kept it short.

"All these charges are small—a pair of pants and boots. I forgave him for more. But the verdict is in now and we can't change it.

We must search ourselves to be fair in the punishing. Just dismissing him out of the service should be punishment enough. No brig time is needed." The captain thanked me and asked for a minute to come to a punishment decision. He then sentenced him to immediate dismissal out of the navy with no further punishment. The accused received the punishment he asked for in prayer with me a week ago. The crew got rid of this guy like they wanted. I didn't get myself in any major trouble. So everything worked out.

A day later, we arrived back at our homeport. After we had moored, I headed for the pay phone. When I was headed back to the ship, I ran into the other two guys who had charged the accused. We talked for a minute about the verdict. The guy with the pants was furious that the guy got off so easily. He was angry about the outcome. He wanted him in prison. After he vented about it, he walked off. The guy with the stolen boots walked on with me. He told me that he respected me and asked how I could forgive someone so quickly. He couldn't believe how I withstood the pressure to testify. He shared that he had to search the Koran for scriptures to support forgiveness for stealing. He did find some eventually, but he was impressed that I automatically forgave, especially since I took the biggest loss. I explained to him that God did the same for us. He took the biggest loss by giving up His Son, Jesus Christ, for us sinners. The Muslim replied that he finally understood the impact of that story. He thanked me for being a good person and showing him forgiveness instead of revenge or justice. I told him there was no justice in forgiveness. When we forgive, we require no payment or restitution. There was no way we could ever pay God back for the gift of His Son, Jesus Christ. I was glad that I started a stir in his heart to question the belief system that he had chosen. I told him that he needed to believe everything in his faith to be in it. I shared with him how I had no doubt about the God I served and the involvement He has in my life. He agreed with me that I was a person who God's hand was on. He then left back to the ship.

I stopped at the end of the pier and stared into at the water and the night lights reflecting on it. I thanked God for an amazing week of protection.

14

ONE LAST MIRACLE
BEFORE I LEAVE

The ship was scheduled for a test of our damage control readiness. We picked up some inspectors in San Diego to evaluate us over the next week at sea. It was an important test. Previous ships that failed this test were considered unfit for duty. Stories about failures ranged from replacing the commanding officer and executive officer to replacing the entire crew. Since we all had damage control responsibilities besides our regular jobs, we were working twice as hard each day. I was part of the main hose team. We were the first men on the scene of a shipboard fire. I was on the water main but rotated through the line for each position on the hose. I was the last man on the rotation. My job was to keep the water flowing, the AFFF (Aqueous Fire Fighting Foam) filled, and straighten the lines. We trained everyday with our teams until lights out about 2130 (9:30 P.M.) before taps. We also trained in every scenario of onboard catastrophe imaginable. We simulated numerous fires in every compartment and missile hits throughout the entire ship. We even practiced responding to chemical leaks that killed us while we slept. We had people's hands, legs, bodies, and heads being cut off in front of us. Crewmembers were electrocuted, drowned, shot, and set on fire to see how we would respond. No matter the scenario, we practiced it to the best of our ability.

When the inspectors came aboard, we were not that good. We kept messing up almost on every drill. We would take too long to put fires out. The ship sank two or three times. Crewmembers were scattered throughout the ship, lying on the floor dead. We were left with only two or three people alive to fight fires and floods. We even had one-legged sailors hopping around carrying fire hoses. It was a mess. These inspectors showed no mercy. They twisted each scenario into a bigger crisis every minute. We didn't have anything left to give. I think the crew overworked themselves practicing. Our first-round grades were low. The second round was a little better. The third round was crucial, but we scored less on that round than the previous two rounds. All the crew knew that we were failing the exam. In fact, the trip back to Long Beach was very quiet. Not many people moved about the ship. I happened to be on the mess decks watching a Christian TV program, just relaxing and reading my Bible, when the captain came by the mess decks. He snickered at what I was watching. Then he sat down on the table opposite me.

"Padre. Can I talk to you for a minute?" he asked. "I just talked to the inspectors and it doesn't look good. We failed the fire readiness test three times." He looked down at my Bible and grabbed the side of the binding. "Maybe you could say a little prayer for us tonight. We need a miracle before we moor up to the pier back home."

"Let's pray right now, captain," I answered.

I had seen it many times in my life as a minister. God will give a new believer a shock of faith by granting his first prayer. It doesn't happen all the time, but it had happened enough times that I felt confident in suggesting it to him.

The captain looked puzzled. Then he replied, "Sure, why not?"

I prayed a simple short prayer asking God to provide a miracle and favor with the inspectors. Then I asked God to touch the captain because of his heart for the crew. The captain said thank you and walked off.

This was exciting! I knew God would do something for this man. The captain had always been fair to me and at times favored me in situations. He gave me a half-dozen commendations under his command. Plus, he gave me respect and respected my faith in God. That night I prayed the night through.

In the morning, I stood on the forward part of the ship as we were getting lines ready for mooring to the pier. The shore was getting closer by the minute. The captain looked over from the outside of the pilothouse, staring at me as if I had a button to push and make something happen. As time went on, the captain seemed to be getting more nervous. He called me over to talk to him from outside the pilothouse. My chief told me to keep working. The captain yelled to my chief that he needed me for a second. Chief seemed suspicious, but let me go.

Looking up three levels, I waited.

"When is it going to happen?" he said.

I was surprised that he actually believed. "Soon," I replied. "But I need somewhere to pray."

"Go find it. Now."

Just then, my chief came over to get me back to work.

The captain intervened. "I need Yanez to get something from downstairs."

The chief smirked. "So now you're the captain's boy, huh?"

Eventually, he let me go. I jumped down one of the scuttles where we stowed the lines. People were working in there so I couldn't pray there. There was no place to go except farther down below. I went down another deck, which ended up just outside the sonar room. I figured this was best place to pray. My prayer went something like this, "Dad. I need you to help my captain right now. He came to you believing that you could help. I know from experience that a person's first genuine request is usually a 'gimme' anyway. Please, Father, we need something to happen, because we are almost to port. Let his faith be touched right now."

Every alarm went off on the ship. I smiled. "Thanks, Lord!" I said aloud as I ran to my emergency post. A fuel fire was spreading through engines one and two. The inspectors started to grab the fire gear to put the fire out, but crew pushed them out of the way. We took our positions. Some of the guys were yelling at the inspectors that this was still our ship.

All over the ship, we fought the fire until it was out. When we knew the fire was extinguished, we continued on our way to moor in Long Beach. After we had moored, the inspectors quickly left the ship, no doubt glad to be back on land and away from us.

It was deathly quiet on the ship. We all knew we had failed the inspection. Then the captain's voice came through the speaker system. "Gentlemen," he said, "we knew this was going to be a hard task to complete. We even knew we were going to be pushed to the limits. This ship responded with dedication, courage, and teamwork throughout every test, even when it was obvious that we had failed. You went on to surprise everyone by saving this ship from a real catastrophe off the coast of our homeport. Gentlemen, with your hard work, commitment, and a miracle, we passed the inspection. I want to thank God for this miracle and your courage. Amen."

The ship was silent no more. We all began jumping up and screaming in excitement. We rushed around to finish our duties so we could celebrate. I joined the rest of the crew for trash detail in one of the helicopter hangers where we grabbed plastic bags full of accumulated trash and walked them to huge dumpsters on the pier. As I came back on the ship, someone pulled me through to the other helicopter hangers. It was the captain. He was just staring at me, so I figured I should salute him. As I started to, he slapped my hand down and said, "Tell your God that I salute Him and thank you." Then the captain saluted me.

I returned the salute, fighting back a goofy smile that wanted to spread across my face. "Captain, we could tell him together right now."

"Don't push it, Padre. Not yet, but soon." He then walked off. A month later, the captain was promoted to a destroyer battle group in Hawaii. The executive officer was acting captain while we moved to San Diego. The base was shutting down in Long Beach.

Three months later, on May 27, 1993, I heard the bell ring for me as I walked off the quarterdeck for the last time. My friend was ringing me out. This salute was usually reserved for officers only. He rang the bell twice then announced over the microphone, "Seaman David Yanez, United States Navy, departing." Then he gave me a single bell known as the stinger. I saluted the ship's flag one last time and turned around to walk across the bow for the last time. When I got to the middle of the bow, I lifted up my hands to heaven. With a loud voice I screamed with all my heart, "Thank you, Jesus! I finally made it. Hallelujah, Hallelujah, Hallelujah!"

CONCLUSION

Dressed in my bell-bottomed dungarees, I stood my night watches dreaming of preaching in services around the world. But the desire to serve God grew even stronger while I served my country, even to the point that I went out to preach in whatever ports we visited. I sometimes thought I might be missing my chance to do the work of God because I was in the navy. Today, I can see that God had a purpose for me to be there.

This book is full of my personal testimonies and my experiences of faith while in the navy. It is also a glimpse into my ministry training ground, the place where I spent hours praying, fasting, and studying.

If you are a soldier, I pray this book encouraged you and offered proof that a strong relationship with God is possible while serving your country. Your walk with God doesn't need to be compromised because of the uniform you wear. Faith is important in the military, especially because of the dangers, tragedies, and losses that can occur at anytime while we serve.

A few years ago, I ran into a former shipmate of mine. We had both been out of the military for at least a dozen years. He was surprise to see that I was still serving God. He had believed that my faith was just a crutch to help me deal with the military life. He then went on to say that he realized I must have really loved the Lord, because I was just as excited talking about God today as I was back in the navy years.

I'd like to share a few things that helped me get through the military service and still be in love with God twenty years later. First, I had a great support system on the ship. Several men of God—preachers and active church members—modeled daily Christian living onboard the ship. These men were in love with their faith! We were constantly encouraging one another. Second, I made a daily effort to read and pray. Even after those hard training days, I spent time with God. It was during these alone times with God that I truly learned to hear Him. Third, I plugged myself into a good home church wherever I was stationed. Fortunately for me, I spent most my time in Southern California. So I was close to my home church, Calvary Assembly of God in Cerritos, California. My church home gave me an instant family of faith. That helped with the loneliness I felt as a serviceman far away from his family. A home church keeps you active, creates good relationships, and keeps you accountable. I also made good Christian friends outside the base and church. This gave me other places to visit and to grow my spiritual life. Whenever I had a chance on any port visit, I would spend time looking for a church service. Last, I lived my life openly for God. No matter the persecution or ridicule, I loved Jesus. I wasn't a holy roller, but people knew I was a Christian. I didn't bend to the world or compromise my faith. The point is, if you keep focused, motivated, and sensitive to God, He will open up doors for you. These doors will lead you to some of the greatest relationships of faith you will ever have.

God Bless,
David Yanez

WHERE IS THE REV NOW?

Pastor David Yanez, "The Rev," has been preaching the gospel since he was sixteen years old. God has used him in the U.S. Navy, throughout our nation, and many places in the world to deliver healing, hope, and the gospel of salvation.

In his early twenties, he interned with a mission ministry from India to help reach the 1.5 billion in India and Asia that do not know Jesus.

In his early thirties, he started hosting a popular radio show called *Midwatch with the Rev*. Thousands of people from coast to coast have listened online and over the airwaves.

Today, The Rev continues in ministry as a pastor, author, radio/TV host, missionary, and evangelist through Revelation Ministries, a 501c(3) tax-exempt non-profit organization.

He holds healing services, relationship conferences, and speaking engagements around the nation through David Yanez Ministries. He is the station general manager for RevMedia Network and director of RevMedia Publishing, all of which he founded.

Thousands have heard the gospel through David Yanez Ministries crusades, pastors' conferences, and helps ministries. Through RevLife, David Yanez has built several orphanages and a Bible college in India, in addition to a preschool in Kenya.

In 2011, RevMedia Network reached 2.5 million listeners and active users after just two and a half years of broadcasting. Also in 2011, RevMedia Publishing successfully released its fifteenth book title. Currently, nine authors have published through RevMedia.

The Rev's desire is to reach the world with the gospel. He feels that can be best accomplished through all these activities combined. If you would like to become part of a dynamic ministry that has a heart for evangelizing, please contact:

REVELATION MINISTRIES
PO BOX 5172
KINGWOOD, TX 77325

david@revministries.com
www.revmedianetwork.com
www.revministries.com
www.revmediapublishing.com
www.davidyanezministries.com
www.revmediatv.com

"For a dream cometh through the multitude of business…"
(Ecclesiastes 5:3)

MILITARY SUPPORT INFORMATION

HOTLINES AND FAMILY SUPPORT INFORMATION NUMBERS

ARMY
1-800-833-6622

AIR FORCE
1-800-435-9941

NAVY
1-800-FSCLINE or 1-800-372-5463

MARINE CORPS
For marines stationed East of the Mississippi River
(minus Wisconsin) 1-800-253-1624

For Marines stationed West of the Mississippi River
(plus Wisconsin) 1-800-253-1624

NATIONAL GUARD BUREAU
1-888-777-7731 (Headquarters NGB)

Defense Logistics Agency (DLA)
1-800-222-0364

US COAST GUARD
1-800-872-4957, EXT 932

DEPLOYMENT HEALTH SUPPORT HOTLINE
1-800-497-6261

www.militaryhomefront.dod.mil
www.militaryonesource.mil
www.uso.org
www.familiesnearandfar.org
www.cmfhq.org
www.cmwives.org

PRAYER LINES
RevMediaNetwork/RevMedia TV
1-888-642-4767 ext 4

TBN
714-731-1000

Daystar
1-800-329-0029

OTHER BOOKS
BY DAVID YANEZ

Almost Out Of Grace

"Have you ever felt that you let God down in your dating or marriage relationships? Sometimes you may have felt like that you have done this all over again. If fact you get a déjà vu feeling. You feel you let God down so much that you're almost out of grace. If so I have written this book for you."

www.almostoutofgrace.com

Visit us for other books by RevMedia Publishing
www.revmediapublishing.com

SALVATION PRAYER

Life is not as complicated as most people think. If you are in covenant with Jesus, all you have to do is please Him and everything else takes care of itself. Trust in God and make Him your source of supply and by faith you can live on earth like it is in heaven.

> *Therefore take no thought, saying, What shall we eat? or, What shall we drink or, Wherewithal shall we be clothed? (for after all these things do the Gentiles seek) for your heavenly Father knoweth that ye have need of all these things. But seek ye first the kingdom of God, and his righteousness; and all these things shall be added unto you.* (Matthew 6:31–33)

Those that have entered into a blood covenant with God by being born again by the spirit of God have eternal life and can walk in health and prosper.

> *Beloved, I wish above all things that thou mayest prosper and be in health, even as thy soul prospereth.* (3 John 2)

Remember, God does not automatically heal and prosper you. We have to call upon His promises in the name of Jesus. Every good thing comes to us through Jesus. The only qualification to receive from the Father is that we know His Jesus. We have to have made Jesus our Lord and Savior.

Everyone needs Jesus because our sins have separated us from a holy God. There is not anyone who has not told a lie or committed a sin. God, however, is holy and cannot fellowship with sin.

So He sent His son, Jesus, to be a man and pay for our sins that we might have the righteousness of God.

Jesus took on our sins and by faith we can receive the exchange of His righteousness and therefore boldly enter into the throne of grace. It's not based on what we have done but what Jesus has done for us. If you will receive Jesus, you will never have to be ashamed again, for Jesus will not be ashamed of you.

> *For both he that sanctifieth and they who are sanctified are all of one: for which cause he is not ashamed to call them brethren.* (Hebrews 2:11)

Because of the sin of Adam, we stand condemned until we receive Jesus by faith. Jesus did not come into the world to condemn the world but to set us free from the condemnation we are already in. It is a free gift of God. We simply receive it by faith.

> *Therefore as by the offence of the judgment came upon all men to condemnation: even so by the righteousness of one free gift upon all men unto justification of life. For as by one man's disobedience many were made sinners, so by the obedience of one shall many be made righteous. Moreover the law entered, that the offence might abound. But where sin abounded, grace did much more abound: that as sin hath reigned unto death, even so might grace reign through righteousness unto eternal life by Jesus Christ our Lord.* (Romans 5:18–21)

If you have never received Jesus into your heart but you would like to, then pray this prayer and mean it in your heart. You will inherit eternal life and can begin walking in your inheritance by receiving provision and health on this earth in the name of Jesus.

Lord Jesus, I am a sinner. Forgive me of my sins, come into my heart and make me brand new. Wash me clean in your precious blood. I confess you as my Lord and Savior and I will serve you all the days of my life. Jesus, thank you for saving me and I thank you that I am now a child of God and my name is written in heaven. I thank you that I now can call upon your name for healing and provision. Help me to make you my source of supply for every area of my life. AMEN

Please contact us to let us know that you prayed this prayer so we can agree with you and rejoice together.

david@davidyanezministries.com

PRAYER FOR HEALING

Jesus wants you healed. All we have to do is ask and believe His Word.

> *And Jesus departed from thence, and came nigh unto the Sea of Galilee; and went up into a mountain, and sat down there. And great multitudes came unto him, having with them those that were lame, blind, dumb, maimed, and many others, and cast them down at Jesus' feet; and he healed them: insomuch that the multitude wondered, when they saw the dumb to speak, the maimed to be whole, the lame to walk, and the blind to see: and they glorified the God of Israel.*
> (Matthew 15:29–31)

You see, it's the healing that glorifies God, sickness only glorifies the devil. You can still glorify God when you are sick but God is never glorified in sickness. Great multitudes came to Jesus and He healed them all. To me a multitude of people is as many people as the eye can see. A great multitude of people is more than that. Great multitudes are even more than that. Yet Jesus did not turn even one person away but healed them all.

Some people think that God won't heal them because of some bad things they have done. Healing is for whosoever will receive it by faith. It is not based on performance. Don't you think that in great multitudes that there is at least one person whose performance is worse than yours? Yet, Jesus healed them.

In great multitudes you will find every kind of person. You'll find rich and poor, young and old, and every ethnic background.

In great multitudes, there are educated people and those with no schooling, people from good families and people from bad families. There are those that are married, singled, and divorced. There are people with religious training and people who have never even prayed before. There are kind people and mean people. There are people who are sexually pure and those that have performed perversion. There are all kinds of people. Jesus healed them all.

God desires greatly for us to receive our healing. Jesus took thirty-nine stripes on His back so that we could be healed. Jesus will never say no to your healing. If Jesus wanted to say no, He wouldn't have had to take one stripe. He didn't take stripes on His back to say no, He took the stripes so that He could say, YES! Pray this prayer out loud and believe God for healing.

Father,

I come to you in the name of Jesus. I give you thanks that by your stripes I was healed and I receive it now by faith. I speak God life and resurrection power into my body to make me whole from the top of my head to the soles of my feet for the glory of God. I release my faith for it and count it as already done in the name of Jesus. Amen.